# Sexual Perversity
# in Chicago

AND

# The Duck
# Variations

WORKS BY DAVID MAMET
PUBLISHED BY GROVE PRESS

*Plays*
American Buffalo
Glengarry Glen Ross
Goldberg Street: Short Plays and Monologues
A Life in the Theatre
Reunion *and* Dark Pony
Sexual Perversity in Chicago *and* The Duck Variations
Speed-the-Plow
The Shawl *and* Prairie du Chien
Three Children's Plays
    The Poet and the Rent
    The Frog Prince
    The Revenge of the Space Pandas or Binky Rudich and the
        Two-Speed Clock
The Woods, Lakeboat, Edmond

*Screenplays*
Five Television Plays
    A Waitress in Yellowstone
    Branford
    The Museum of Science and Industry Story
    A Wasted Weekend
    We Will Take You There
Homicide
House of Games
Things Change *(with Shel Silverstein)*
We're No Angels

*Adaptations by David Mamet*
The Cherry Orchard, by Anton Chekhov
The Three Sisters, by Anton Chekhov
Uncle Vanya, by Anton Chekhov

# Sexual Perversity in Chicago

AND

# The Duck Variations

TWO PLAYS BY
David Mamet

Grove Press
New York

*Published simultaneously in Canada*
*Printed in the United States of America*

Library of Congress Cataloging-in-Publication Data

Mamet, David.
  Sexual perversity in Chicago and The duck variations.

  I. Mamet, David. The duck variations. 1978.  II. Title: Sexual perversity in Chicago.
PS3563.A4345S4    1978    812'.5'4    77-91885
ISBN-10: 0-8021-5011-X
ISBN-13: 978-0-8021-5011-0

Grove Press
an imprint of Grove/Atlantic, Inc.
841 Broadway
New York, NY  10003

Distributed by Publishers Group West

www.groveatlantic.com

07 08 09 10    30 29 28 27 26 25 24 23

# Sexual
# Perversity
# in
# Chicago

This play is dedicated to Jonathan Katz, with thanks for his comradeship, understanding, and most of the good lines.

*Sexual Perversity in Chicago* was first produced by The Organic Theater Company, Chicago, Illinois, in the summer of 1974, with the following cast:

| | |
|---|---|
| BERNARD | Warren Casey |
| DAN | Eric Loeb |
| DEBORAH | Carolyn Gordon |
| JOAN | Roberta Custer |

This production was directed by Stuart Gordon; set by John Paoletti and Mary Griswold; lighting by Jeffrey Buschor.

It was produced off-off Broadway at St. Clements Theatre, New York City, in December of 1975, with the following cast:

| | |
|---|---|
| BERNARD | Robert Townsend |
| DAN | Robert Picardo |
| DEBORAH | Jane Anderson |
| JOAN | Gina Rogers |

This production was directed by Albert Takazauckas; set by Michael Massee; lighting by Gary Porto.

It opened off-Broadway at the Cherry Lane Theatre, New York City, in June of 1976, produced by Larry Goossen and Jeffrey Wachtel, with the following cast;

| | |
|---|---|
| BERNARD | F. Murray Abraham |
| DAN | Peter Riegert |
| DEBORAH | Jane Anderson |
| JOAN | Gina Rogers |

This production was directed by Albert Takazauckas; set by Michael Massee; lighting by Gary Porto.

# The Characters:

DAN SHAPIRO         An urban male in his late twenties.

BERNARD LITKO      A friend and associate of Dan Shapiro.

DEBORAH SOLOMAN    A woman in her late twenties.

JOAN WEBBER        Friend and roommate of Deborah Soloman.

# The Scene:

Various spots around the North Side of Chicago, a Big City on a Lake.

# The Time:

Approximately nine weeks one summer.

*A singles bar.* DAN SHAPIRO and BERNARD LITKO are seated at the bar.

DANNY: So how'd you do last night?

BERNIE: Are you kidding me?

DANNY: Yeah?

BERNIE: Are you fucking kidding me?

DANNY: Yeah?

BERNIE: Are you pulling my leg?

DANNY: So?

BERNIE: So tits out to here so.

DANNY: Yeah?

BERNIE: Twenty, a couple years old.

DANNY: You gotta be fooling.

BERNIE: Nope.

DANNY: You devil.

BERNIE: You think she hadn't been around?

DANNY: Yeah?

BERNIE: She hadn't gone the route?

DANNY: She knew the route, huh?

BERNIE: Are you fucking kidding me?

DANNY: Yeah?

BERNIE: So *wrote* the route.

DANNY: No shit, around twenty, huh?

BERNIE: Nineteen, twenty.

DANNY: You're talking about a girl.

BERNIE: Damn right.

DANNY: You're telling me about some underage stuff.

BERNIE: She don't gotta be but eighteen.

DANNY: Was she?

BERNIE: Shit yes.

DANNY: Then okay.

BERNIE: She made eighteen easy.

DANNY: Well, then.

BERNIE: Had to punch in at twenty, twenty-five easy.

DANNY: Then you got no problem.

BERNIE: I know I got no problem.

DANNY: So tell me.

BERNIE: So okay, so where am I?

DANNY: When?

BERNIE: Last night, two-thirty.

DANNY: So two-thirty, you're probably over at Yak-Zies.

BERNIE: Left Yak-Zies at one.

DANNY: So you're probably over at Grunts.

BERNIE: They only got a two o'clock license.

DANNY: So you're probably over at the Commonwealth.

BERNIE: So okay, so I'm over at the Commonwealth, in the pancake house off the lobby, and I'm working on a stack of those raisin and nut jobs . . .

DANNY: They're good.

BERNIE: . . . and I'm reading the paper, and I'm reading, and I'm casing the pancake house, and the usual shot, am I right?

DANNY: Right.

BERNIE: So who walks in over to the cash register but this chick.

DANNY: Right.

BERNIE: Nineteen-, twenty-year-old chick . . .

DANNY: Who we're talking about.

BERNIE: . . . and she wants a pack of Viceroys.

DANNY: I can believe that.

BERNIE: Gets the smokes, and she does this number about how she forgot her purse up in her room.

DANNY: Up in her room?

BERNIE: Yeah.

DANNY: Was she a pro?

BERNIE: At that age?

DANNY: Yeah.

BERNIE: Well, at this point we don't know. So anyway, I go over and ask her can I front her for the smokes, and she says she couldn't, and then she says Well, all right, and would I like to join her in a cup of coffee.

DANNY: She asked you . . .

BERNIE: . . . yeah.

DANNY: For a cup of coffee?

BERNIE: Right?

DANNY: And all this time she was nineteen?

BERNIE: Nineteen, twenty. So down we sit and get to talking. This, that, blah, blah, blah, and "Come up to my room and I'll pay you back for the cigarettes."

DANNY: No.

BERNIE: Yeah.

DANNY: You're shitting me.

BERNIE: I'm telling you.

DANNY: And was she a pro?

BERNIE: So at this point, we don't know. Pro, semi-pro, Betty Coed from College, regular young broad, it's anybody's ballgame. So, anyway, up we go. Fifth floor on the alley and it's "Sit down, you wanna drink?" "What you got?", "Bourbon," "Fine." And goddam if she doesn't lay half a rock on me for the cigarettes.

DANNY: No.

BERNIE: Yeah.

DANNY: So this changes the complexity of things.

BERNIE: For a bit, yes. But *then* what shot does she up and pull?

DANNY: You remind her of her ex.

BERNIE: No.

DANNY: She's never done anything like this before in her life?

BERNIE: No.

DANNY: She just got into town, and do you know where a girl like her could make a little money?

BERNIE: No.

DANNY: So I'm not going to lie to you, what shot does she pull?

BERNIE: The shot she is pulling is the following two things: (a) she says "I think I want to take a shower."

DANNY: No.

BERNIE: Yes. And (b) she says "And then let's fuck."

DANNY: Yeah?

BERNIE: What did I just tell you?

DANNY: She said that?

BERNIE: I hope to tell you.

DANNY: Nineteen years old?

BERNIE: Nineteen, twenty.

DANNY: And was she a pro?

BERNIE: So at this point I don't know. But I do say I'll join her in the shower, if she has no objections.

DANNY: Of course.

BERNIE: So into the old shower. And does this broad have a *body?*

DANNY: Yeah?

BERNIE: Are you kidding me?

DANNY: So tell me.

BERNIE: The *tits* . . .

DANNY: Yeah?

BERNIE: The *legs* . . .

DANNY: The ass?

BERNIE: Are you fucking fooling me? The *ass* on this broad . . .

DANNY: Young ass, huh?

BERNIE: Well yeah, young broad, young ass.

DANNY: Right.

BERNIE: And lathering her . . .

DANNY: Mmmm.

BERNIE: And drop the *soap* . . . This, that, and we get out. Toweling off, each of us in his or her full glory. So while we're toweling off, I flick the towel at her, very playfully, and by accident it catches her a good one on the ass, and *thwack*, a big red mark.

DANNY: No.

BERNIE: So I'm all sorry and so forth. But what does this broad do but let out a squeal of pleasure and relief that would fucking kill a horse.

DANNY: Huh?

BERNIE: So what the hell, I'm liberal.

DANNY: If that's her act, that's her act.

BERNIE: Goes without saying. So I look around, figuring to follow in my footsteps, and what is handy but this little G.E. clock radio. So I pick the mother up and heave it at her. Catches her across the shoulder blades, and we've got this long welt.

DANNY: Draw blood?

BERNIE: At this point, no. So what does she do? She says "wait a minute," and she crawls under the bed. From under the bed she pulls this suitcase, and from out of the suitcase comes this World War II Flak Suit.

DANNY: They're hard to find.

BERNIE: Zip, zip, zip, and she gets into the Flak Suit and we get down on the bed.

DANNY: What are you doing?

BERNIE: Fucking.

DANNY: She's in the Flak Suit?

BERNIE: Right.

DANNY: How do you get in?

BERNIE: How do you think I get in? She leaves the zipper open.

DANNY: That's what I thought.

BERNIE: But the shot is, while we're fucking, she wants me, every thirty seconds or so, to go BOOM at the top of my lungs.

DANNY: At her?

BERNIE: No, just in general. So we're humping and bumping and greasing the old Flak Suit and every once in a while I go BOOM, and she starts in on me. "Turn me over," she says, so I do. She's on her stomach. I'm on top. . . .

DANNY: They got a flap in the back of the Flak Suit?

BERNIE: Yes. So she's on her stomach, et cetera. In the middle of everything she slithers over to the side of the bed, picks up the house phone and says "Give me Room 511."

DANNY: Right.

BERNIE: "Who are you calling?" I say. "A friend," she says. So okay. They answer the phone. "Patrice," she says, "It's me, I'm up here with a friend, and I could use a little help. Could you help me out?"

DANNY: Ah ha!

BERNIE: So wait. So I don't know what the shot is. So all of a sudden I hear coming out of the phone: "Rat Tat Tat Tat Tat. Ka POW! AK AK AK AK AK AK AK *Ka Pow!*" So fine. I'm pumping away, the chick on the other end is making airplane noises, every once in a while I go BOOM, and the broad on the bed starts going crazy. She's moaning and groaning and about to go the whole long route. Humping and bumping, and she's screaming "Red dog One to Red dog Squadron" . . . all of a sudden she screams "Wait." She wriggles out, leans under the bed, and she pulls out this five-gallon jerrycan.

DANNY: Right.

BERNIE: Opens it up . . . it's full of gasoline. So she splashes the mother all over the walls, whips a fuckin' Zippo out of the Flak suit, and WHOOSH, the whole room is in flames. So the whole fuckin' joint is going up in smoke, the telephone is going "Rat Tat Tat," the broad jumps back on the bed and yells "Now, give it to me *now* for the love of Christ." *(Pause.)* So I look at the broad . . . and I figure . . . fuck this nonsense. I grab my clothes, I peel a sawbuck off my wad, as I make the door I fling it at her. "For cab fare," I yell. She doesn't hear nothing. One, two, six, I'm in the hall. Struggling into my shorts and hustling for the elevator. Whole fucking hall is full of smoke, above the flames I just make out my broad, she's singing "Off we go into the Wild Blue Yonder," and the elevator arrives, and the whole fucking hall is full of *firemen. (Pause.)* Those fucking firemen make out like bandits. *(Pause.)*

DANNY: Nobody does it normally anymore.

BERNIE: It's these young broads. They don't know what the fuck they want.

DANNY: You think she was a pro?

BERNIE: A pro, Dan . . .

DANNY: Yes.

BERNIE: . . . is how you think about yourself. You see my point?

DANNY: Yeah.

BERNIE: Well, all right, then. I'll tell you one thing . . . she knew all the pro moves.

JOAN *and* DEB *at the apartment that they share.* JOAN *is getting ready to go out.*

JOAN: Men.

DEBORAH: Yup.

JOAN: They're all after only one thing.

DEBORAH: Yes. I know. *(Pause.)*

JOAN: But it's never the *same* thing.

JOAN *is at a singles bar seated alone.* BERNARD *spots her and moves to her table.*

BERNIE: Evening. Good evening.

JOAN: Good evening.

BERNIE: How would you like some company. *(Pause.)* What if I was to sit down here? What would that do for you, huh?

JOAN: No, I don't think so, no.

*Pause.*

Is there something I can do for you?

BERNIE: Nope. Not a thing in the world, no. I'm just *standing* here, looking for some place to sit down, huh? *(Pause. Sits down at her table.)*

Well, is it a free country, or what?

JOAN: Don't torture me, just let me hear it, okay?

BERNIE *(Pause)*: So here I am. I'm just in town for a one-day layover and I happen to find myself in this bar. So, so far so good. What am I going to do? I could lounge alone and lonely and stare into my drink, or I could take the bull by the horns and make an effort to enjoy myself . . .

JOAN: Are you making this up?

BERNIE: So hold on. So I see you seated at this table and I say to myself, "Doug McKenzie, there is a young woman," I say to myself, "What is she doing here?", and I think she is here for the same reasons as I. To enjoy herself, and perhaps, to meet provocative people. *(Pause.)* I'm a meteorologist for TWA. It's an incredibly interesting, but lonely job. . . . Stuck in the cockpit of some jumbo jet hours at a time . . . nothing to look at but charts . . . What are you drinking?

JOAN: Scotch on the rocks.

BERNIE: You're a scotch drinker, huh?

JOAN: Yes.

BERNIE: Well, what the hell, you're drinking scotch. But I say "Why pigeonhole ourselves?" A person makes an effort to enjoy himself, why pin a label on it, huh? This is life. You learn a lot about life working for the airlines. Because you're constantly in touch, you know with what?, with the idea of Death. *(Pause.)* Not that I'm a fan of morbidness, and so on. I mean what are you doing here? You're by yourself, I can see that. So what do you come here for? To what?

To meet interesting new people or not. *(Pause.)* What else is there?

JOAN: Can I tell you something?

BERNIE: You bet.

JOAN: Forgive me if I'm being too personal . . . but I do not find you sexually attractive. *(Pause.)*

BERNIE: What is that, some new kind of line? Huh? I mean, not that I mind what you think, if that's what you think . . . but . . . that's a fucking rotten thing to say.

JOAN: I'll live.

BERNIE: All kidding aside . . . lookit, I'm a fucking professional, huh? My life is a bunch of having to make split-second decisions. Life or death fucking decisions. So that's what it is, so okay. I work hard, I play hard. Comes I got a day off I wanna relax a bit . . . I wander—quite by accident—into this bar. I have a drink or two . . . perhaps a drop too much. Perhaps I get *too* loose (it's been known to happen).° So what do I see? A nice young woman sitting by herself . . .

JOAN: We've done this one.

BERNIE: So just who the fuck do you think you are, God's gift to Women? I mean where do you fucking get off with this shit. You don't want to get come on to, go enroll in a convent. You think I don't have better things to do? I don't have better ways to spend my off hours than to listen to some nowhere cunt try out cute bits on me? I mean why don't you just clean

---

° Some portions of the dialogue appear in parentheses, which serve to mark a slight change of outlook on the part of the speaker—perhaps a momentary change to a more introspective regard.—D.M.

your fucking act up, Missy. You're living in a city in 1976. (*Pause.*) Am I getting through to you?

JOAN: I think I'd like to be left alone.

BERNIE: Ah, you're breaking my heart. My fucking heart is pumping pisswater for you. You're torturing me with your pain and aloofness. You know that?

JOAN: I'm terribly sorry.

BERNIE: Sorry don't mean shit. You're a grown woman, behave like it for chrissakes. Huh? I mean, what the fuck do you think society is, just a bunch of rules strung together for your personal pleasure?

JOAN: Sometimes I think I'm not a very nice person.

BERNIE: You flatter yourself. (JOAN *rises.*) So where are you going now?

JOAN: My little boy is sick, and I really should be getting home.

BERNIE: Cockteaser.

JOAN: I beg your pardon?

BERNIE: You heard me.

JOAN: I have never been called that in my life.

BERNIE: Well, you just lost your cherry.

JOAN: I . . . I find that very insulting.

BERNIE: Go get a lawyer, bitch. Go get a writ, you got yourself a case.

(*Pause.*)

JOAN (*sits down again*): I . . . I'm . . . I'm sorry if I was being rude to you.

BERNIE: Oh, you're sorry if you were being rude to me.

JOAN: Yes.

BERNIE: You got a lot of fuckin' nerve. *(Rises, calls for check, exits.)*

*At work.* DAN *and* BERNARD *are at work. They are filing.*

BERNIE: The main thing, Dan . . .

DANNY: Yes?

BERNIE: The main thing about *broads* . . .

DANNY: Yes?

BERNIE: Is two things. One: The Way to Get Laid is to Treat 'Em Like Shit . . .

DANNY: Yeah . . .

BERNIE: . . . and Two: Nothing . . . *nothing* makes you so attractive to the opposite sex as getting your rocks off on a regular basis.

*The Library.* DEB *is seated, working.* DAN *cruises her and so on.*

DANNY: Hi.

DEBORAH: Hello.

DANNY: I saw you at the Art Institute.

DEBORAH: Uh huh.

DANNY: I remembered your hair.

DEBORAH: Hair memory.

DANNY: You were in the Impressionists room. *(Pause.)* Monet... *(Pause.)*

DEBORAH: Uh huh.

DANNY: You're very attractive. I like the way you look. *(Pause.)* You were drawing in charcoal. It was nice. *(Pause.)* Are you a student at the Art Institute?

DEBORAH: No, I work.

DANNY: Work, huh? ... work. *(Pause.)* I'll bet you're good at it. *(Pause.)* Is someone taking up a lot of your time these days?

DEBORAH: You mean a man?

DANNY: Yes, a man.

DEBORAH: I'm a Lesbian. *(Pause.)*

DANNY: As a physical preference, or from political beliefs?

BERNARD's *apartment.* BERNARD *is seated in front of the television at three in the morning.*

TV: When you wish upon a star, makes no difference who you are. If, on the other hand, you apply for a personal loan, all sorts of circumstantial evidence is required. I wonder if any mathematician has done serious research on the efficacity of prayer. For example: you're walking down the street thinking "God, if I don't get laid tonight, I don't know *what* all!" (A common form of prayer) And all of a sudden, WHAM! *(Pause.)* Perhaps you do get laid, or perhaps you get hit by a cab, or perhaps you meet the man or woman of your persuasion. But the prayer is uttered—yes it is—solely as a lamentation, and with no real belief in its causal properties.

When you don't get laid, tomorrow's prayer has the extra added oomph of involuntary continence. But if you do get laid—think on that a moment, will you? If you do manage to moisten the old wick, how many people would stop, before, during or after, and give thanks to a just creator?

DAN *and* DEB *are in bed at his apartment.*

DANNY: Well.

DEBORAH: Well.

DANNY: Yeah, well, hey . . . uh . . . *(Pause.)* I feel *great. (Pause.)* You?

DEBORAH: Uh huh.

DANNY: Yup. *(Pause.)* You, uh, you have to go to work (you work, right?) (DEB *nods.*) You have to go to work tomorrow?

DEBORAH: Yes. Well . . .

DANNY: You're going home?

DEBORAH: Do you want me to?

DANNY: Only if you want to. Do you want to?

DEBORAH: Do you want me to stay? I don't know if it's such a good idea that I stay here tonight.

DANNY: Why? *(Pause.)* I'd like you to stay. If you'd like to.

DEB *nods.*

DANNY: Well, then, all right, then. Huh? *(Pause.)*

DEBORAH: I like your apartment.

DANNY: Yeah? I'm glad.

DEBORAH: I like it here.

DANNY: So, look, so tell me. How would you like to eat dinner with me tomorrow. If you're not doing anything. If you're not too busy. If you're busy it's not important.

DEBORAH: I'd love to eat dinner with you tomorrow.

DANNY: You would, huh?

DEBORAH: Yes.

DANNY: Well, okay, that's nice. That's very nice. I'm going to look forward to that.

DEBORAH: I could come over here and cook.

DANNY: You could.

DEBORAH: Yes.

DANNY: You could come over here and cook dinner, you'd like to do that?

DEBORAH: Yes.

DANNY: We could do that . . .

DEBORAH: Sure.

DANNY: Yeah. We could do that. *(Pause.)* Let's do that.

DEBORAH: Okay. *(Pause.)* I'm not really a Lesbian.

DANNY: No?

DEBORAH: But I have had some Lesbianic experiences.

DANNY: What, like going to bed with other women?

DEBORAH: . . . and I enjoyed them.

DANNY *(pause):* Well, sure. *(Pause.)* You going to sleep?

DEBORAH *(sleepily):* Yes.

DANNY *(Pause):* You having a good time?

DEBORAH *(sleepily):* Yes.

DANNY: That's good. *(Pause.)* Goodnight.

DEBORAH: Goodnight.

> *Pause.*

DANNY: See you in the morning.

> *The next morning.* DEB *and* JOAN *at their apartment.* DEB *enters.*

JOAN: So what's he like?

DEBORAH: Who?

JOAN: Whoever you haven't been home, I haven't seen you in two days that you've been seeing.

DEBORAH: Did you miss me?

JOAN: No. Your plants died. *(Pause.)* I'm kidding. What's his name.

DEBORAH: Danny.

JOAN: What's he do?

DEBORAH: He works in the Loop.

JOAN: How wonderful for him.

DEBORAH: He's an Assistant Office Manager.

JOAN: That's nice, a job with a little upward mobility.

DEBORAH: Don't be like that, Joan.

JOAN: I'm sorry. I don't know what got into me.

DEBORAH: How are things at school?

JOAN: Swell. Life in the Primary Grades is a real picnic. The other kindergarten teacher got raped Tuesday.

DEBORAH: How terrible.

JOAN: What?

DEBORAH: How terrible for her.

JOAN: Well, *of course* it was terrible for her. Good Christ, Deborah, you really amaze me sometimes, you know that?

*A bar.* BERNARD *is seated at the bar; he is waiting.*

BERNIE: What do you have to do to get a drink in this place, come on a cracker?

DAN and DEB *appear at the entrance to the bar.*

DANNY: You're going to like Bernie, you're going to like him a lot. Ah! Ask him to tell you about Korea, he has got some stories you are not going to believe.

BERNARD *spots them.*

BERNIE: Yo! Siddown, siddown, so what are you having?

*They all sit down at a table.*

DANNY: Deborah?

DEBORAH: Jack Daniels on the Rocks.

BERNIE: So she knows what she's talking about, huh? *(To DEB)* Black or Green?

DEBORAH: Black.

BERNIE: *Okay.* And you?

DANNY: The same.

BERNIE: Right back. *(He goes to bar.)*

DANNY: Well, that's Bernie.

DEBORAH: Seems like a nice enough sort of fellow.

DANNY: *Hell* of a guy.

DEBORAH: Is he coming with us to the movies?

BERNARD *comes back with drinks.*

BERNIE: So, actually, I'm Bernard Litko; friend and associate of your pal, Danny. And you're Deborah.

DEBORAH: Deborah Soloman.

BERNIE: Danny's been telling me a lot about you.

DEBORAH: We only met Wednesday.

BERNIE: He talks about you constantly.

DEBORAH: No!

BERNIE: Yes.

DEBORAH: What does he say?

BERNIE: All the usual things.

*Pause.*

DANNY: Bernie was in Korea.

DEBORAH: Really?

BERNIE: Yeah. You see M°A°S°H on TV? *(Pause.)* It all looks like that. There isn't one square inch of Korea that doesn't look like that. *(Pause.)* I'm not kidding. *(Pause.)*

DEBORAH: When were you there?

BERNIE: '67.

DEBORAH: Really? What were you doing in Korea in 1967?

*Pause.*

BERNIE: I'm really not at liberty to talk about it.

*Pause.*

So what do you do?

DEBORAH: I'm an illustrator.

BERNIE: Commercial artist, huh?

DEBORAH: Yes.

BERNIE: Lots of money in that. I mean, that's a hell of a field for a girl.

DANNY: She's very good at it.

BERNIE: I don't doubt it for a second. I mean, *look* at her for chrissakes. You're a very attractive woman. Anybody ever tell you that? *(Pause.)* Huh? *(Pause.)* So okay, so what sign are you?

DEBORAH: Scorpio.

BERNIE: Scorpio, huh? . . . Scorpio . . . how about that.

DEBORAH: What sign are *you?*

BERNIE: Scorpio.

DEBORAH: How about that. Danny's a Scorpio.

BERNIE: You a Scorpio, Dan?

DANNY: Yes. *(Pause.)*

BERNIE: Well, I don't want to say it, but it's a small
  fucking world. *(Pause.)* So you guys are hitting it off,
  huh? The two of you, you're hitting it on/off?

DEBORAH: Well . . .

BERNIE: What the hell, it's early. *(To* DAN*)* You don't even
  know if she's a keeper yet, for chrissakes. You're
  young. What the hell. *(To* DEB*)* How old are you?

DANNY: Bernie, you know you're not supposed to ask a
  woman her age.

BERNIE: Dan, Dan, these are modern times. What do you
  think this is, *the past?* Women are liberated. You got
  a right to be what age you are, and so do I, and so
  does Deborah. *(To* DEB*)* Right?

DEBORAH: Oh, I suppose so.

BERNIE: So what are you? Eighteen . . . nineteen.

DEBORAH: Actually, I'm twenty-three.

BERNIE: Well, you don't look it. *(Pause.)* You know,
  you're a lucky guy, Dan. And I think you know what
  I'm talking about. You are one lucky guy. Yes sir,

you are one fortunate son of a bitch. And I think I know what I'm talking about.

DAN *and* BERNARD *are filing at the office.*

BERNIE: One thing, and I want to tell you that if everybody thought of this, Dan, we could do away with income tax (hand me one of those 12-12's, will ya?), there would be no more war (thanks), and you and I could dwell in Earthly Paradise today. *(Pause.)*

DANNY: What?

BERNIE: Just this:

DANNY: Yeah?

BERNIE: That when she's on her back, her legs are in the air, she's coming like a choo-choo and she's screaming "don't stop" . . .

DANNY: Yeah?

BERNIE: I want you to remember . . .

DANNY: . . . yeah? . . .

BERNIE: That power . . . *(Pause.)* . . . that *power* means *responsibility.* *(Pause.)* Remember that.

DANNY: I will.

*Pause.*

BERNIE: Good.

*Outside* DEB *and* JOAN*'s apartment.* JOAN *is leaving the apartment.* DAN *runs into her in the hall.*

DANNY: Hi.

JOAN: Hello.

DANNY: I'm looking for Deborah.

JOAN: She's not here now.

DANNY: Oh. What is she, out?

JOAN: She's out.

DANNY: I'm supposed to meet her here.

JOAN: Well, she's not here now. *(Pause.)*

DANNY: Well, perhaps we could stand out here and tell each other funny stories until she got back. What do you think?

JOAN: Was she expecting you?

DANNY: I'm supposed to meet her here.

JOAN: You were supposed to meet her here when?

DANNY: Now.

JOAN: What time did she say?

DANNY: Around seven.

JOAN: Well, I'll tell her you stopped by.

DANNY: Wait. Wait. . . . what? Could I have a chair or something? I'll be glad to wait outside the door. Maybe if you just have a stool and a copy of *Boy's Life* or something I could read. *(Pause.)* Why are you being so hostile?

JOAN: I don't like your attitude. *(Pause.)*

DANNY: My name is Danny Shapiro.

JOAN: I know who you are.

DAN *and* BERNARD'*s office. They are filing.*

DANNY: You ever do it in a plane?

BERNIE: Yup.

DANNY: Underwater?

BERNIE: Yup.

DANNY: You ever do it in a movie?

BERNIE: Yes I have, Dan. I believe I have, yes. *(Pause.)* You know what some of 'em like? They like you to get a trifle off the beaten track, if you know what I mean. I had this one chick, she used to have me wrap her in a bicycle chain and lock her to the radiator before she'd let me do it.

DANNY: Yeah?

BERNIE: Spent five happy months with that broad before it got cold. A lot of them. They like you to get off the beaten track.

DANNY: Yeah?

BERNIE: *Oh* yeah. Read your history. The Ancient Greeks . . . the French . . . you heard of King Farouk?

DANNY: Yeah.

BERNIE: King Farouk, now one of the shots, I read, he'd pull into some small town, Dubuque, Peoria . . . he'd go put the make on some waitress.

DANNY: Yeah.

BERNIE: So after work, they'd all go back to her place and start making it.

DANNY: Uh huh.

BERNIE: The shot of it was this: now secretly, while she was still at work, his men would go divert the local railroad . . .

DANNY: Yeah . . .

BERNIE: . . . and lay the tracks so they went right through this chick's house. Right by the headboard of her bed and out again on the main line.

DANNY: Uh huh.

BERNIE: So just as she's ready to come . . .

DANNY: Yeah.

BERNIE: The King gives a signal, his men run a locomotive right through the broad's bedroom.

DANNY: No.

BERNIE: Yeah. The broads loved it. The thing of it was this:

DANNY: Yeah.

BERNIE: King Farouk was a bit kinky. Right?

DANNY: Right.

BERNIE: So get this: There they're humping and bumping . . . the chick's about to come. . . .

DANNY: Yeah.

BERNIE: She hears "Chugga chugga chugga," and then *wham*, the house caves in.

DANNY: Uh huh.

BERNIE: So she sits up in bed, she says "What's that?", the King goes "That, my dear, is a choo-choo" . . .

DANNY: Uh huh.

BERNIE: Then he whacks her on the forehead with a ball-peen hammer.

DANNY: No shit.

BERNIE: Yeah.

*Pause.*

DANNY: How'd he get away with it?

BERNIE: You shitting me? The King had emissaries all over the country, they'd fix it up so it looked like the chick had got hit by a train.

*Pause.*

He'd take care of their families, though.

DANNY: The girls' families.

BERNIE: Yeah. He'd send them a couple g's. A g or two in savings bonds.

*Pause.*

DANNY: He could afford it.

BERNIE: Are you shitting me? The man was king of *Egypt*. *(Pause.)* A *huge* fucking country.

DANNY: Yeah.

BERNIE: An ancient land.

DANNY: Yeah.

*Pause.*

BERNIE: So tell me.

DANNY: What?

BERNIE: How are you getting along with that girl?

DANNY: What girl?

BERNIE: You introduced me to.

DANNY: Deborah?

BERNIE: Deborah, Betty, whatever.

DANNY: Her name's Deborah.

BERNIE: I don't know that? I know what her name is, I'm asking you how you're getting on.

DANNY: We're getting on just fine. *(Pause.)*

BERNIE: That's okay. *(Pause.)* You don't want to talk about it, we won't think about it.

DANNY: I didn't say I didn't want to talk about it.

*Pause.*

BERNIE: Does she give head?

DANNY: What?

BERNIE: To you, I'm saying. Does she give head to *you.*

*Pause.*

Forget it.

DANNY: You want me to do these 12-12's?

BERNIE: Yeah, do'em. Do'em. *(Pause.)*

DANNY: You ever make it with an Oriental?

BERNIE: No. I spent eighteen months in Korea jacking off. Do the 12-12's, huh?

✿

JOAN *and* DEB's *apartment. The evening. They are sitting around.*

JOAN: I don't know, I don't know. I don't know, I don't know. I don't know. *(Pause.)*

DEBORAH: You don't know what?

JOAN: I don't know anything, Deborah, I swear to god, the older I get the less I know. *(Pause.)* It's a puzzle. Our efforts at coming to grips with ourselves . . . in an attempt to become "more human" (which, in itself, is an interesting concept). It has to do with an increased ability to recognize *clues* . . . and the control of energy in the form of *lust* . . . and *desire* (And also in the form of hope) . . .

But a *finite* puzzle. Whose true solution lies, perhaps, in transcending the rules themselves . . . *(Pause.)* . . . and pounding of the fucking pieces into places where they DO NOT FIT AT ALL.

*Pause.*

Those of us who have seen the hands of the Master Magician move a bit too slowly do have a rough time from time to time.

*Pause.*

Some things persist. *(Pause.)*
"Loss" is always possible . . .

*Pause.*

*Phone rings.*

DEBORAH: I'll take it in the other room. *(Exits.)*

DAN *and* BERNARD's *office. Closing up.* DAN *and* BER-
NARD *are securing the office at the end of a day.*

BERNIE: So what are we doing tomorrow, we going to the
beach?

DANNY: I'm seeing Deborah.

BERNIE: Yeah? You getting serious? I mean she seemed
like a hell of a girl, huh? The little I saw of her. Not
too this, not too that . . . very kind of . . . what?
*(Pause.)* Well, what the fuck. I only saw her for a
minute. I mean first impressions of this kind are
often misleading, huh? So what can you tell from
seeing a broad one, two, ten times. You're seeing a
lot of this broad. You getting serious? But what the
fuck, that's your business. Right?

DANNY: Umm.

BERNIE: So what are you guys going to do, maybe . . .
what? Go to the zoo, or shopping? . . . She looked
very intellectual.   ·

DANNY: Um.

BERNIE: That's not always a bad thing.

DANNY: No.

BERNIE: I mean what the fuck, a guy wants to get it on with some broad on a more or less stable basis, who is to say him no. *(Pause.)* A lot of these broads, you know, you just don't know. You know? I mean what with where they've been and all. I mean a young woman in today's society . . . time she's twenty two-three. You don't know *where* the fuck she's been. *(Pause.)* I'm just *talking* to you, you understand.

DAN's *apartment.* DAN *and* DEB *are in bed.*

DANNY: So tell me.

DEBORAH: What?

DANNY: Everything. Tell me the *truth* about everything. Menstruation. I know you're holding out on me.

DEBORAH: It would be hard on me if it got out.

DANNY: I swear.

DEBORAH: It's under our conscious control.

DANNY: I knew it!

DEBORAH: We just do it to drive you crazy with the mess.

DANNY: I just knew it . . .

DEBORAH: Now you tell me some.

DANNY: Name it.

DEBORAH: What does it feel like to have a penis?

DANNY: Strange. Very strange and wonderful.

DEBORAH: Do you miss having tits?

DANNY: To be completely frank with you, that is the stupidest question I ever heard. What man in his right mind would want tits?

DEBORAH: You're right, of course. *(Pause.)* Ask me if I like the taste of come.

DANNY: Do you like the taste of come?

DEBORAH: Do I like the taste of come?

DANNY: Yes.

DEBORAH: Dan, I love the taste of come. It tastes like everything . . . *good* . . . just . . . *coming* out of your cock . . . the Junior Prom . . . an autumn afternoon. . . .

DANNY: It doesn't taste a little bit like Chlorox?

DEBORAH: It *smells* like Chlorox. It tastes like the Junior Prom. *(Pause.)* See what you cheat yourself of?

DANNY: Yes.

DEBORAH: Faggot. *(Pause.)*

DANNY: Do you ever fantasize about making love with other women?

DEBORAH: Do you fantasize when we make love? *(Pause.)* The last time we made love, I fantasized about other women.

DANNY: The last time I masturbated I kept thinking about my left hand.

DEBORAH: Did you?

DANNY: Yes.

DEBORAH: Did you?

DANNY: Yes.

*Pause.*

I love making love with you.

DEBORAH: I love making love with you. *(Pause.)*

DANNY: I love you.

DEBORAH: Does it frighten you to say that?

DANNY: Yes.

DEBORAH: It's only words. I don't think you should be frightened by words.

*Nursery School.* JOAN *is lecturing two toddlers.*

JOAN: What are you doing? Where are you going? What are you doing? You stay right there. Now. What were the two of you doing? I'm just asking a simple question. There's nothing to be ashamed of. *(Pause.)* I can wait. *(Pause.)* Were you playing "Doctor"? *(Pause.)* "Doctor." Don't play dumb with me, just answer the question. (You know, that attitude is going to get you in a lot of trouble someday.) Were you playing with each other's genitals? Each other's . . . "pee-pees"? . . . whatever you call them at home, that's what I'm asking (and don't play dumb, because I saw what you were doing, so just own up to it). *(Pause.)* All right . . . no. No, stop that, there's no reason for tears . . . it's perfectly . . . natural. But . . . there's a time and a place for everything. Now . . . no, it's all right. Come on. Come on, we're all going in the other room, and we're going to wash

our hands. And then Miss Webber is going to call
our parents.

*The Toy Department at Marshall Field's.* BERNARD
*and* DAN *are shopping for a gift.*

DANNY: Whose birthday?

BERNIE: My nephew Bobby.

DANNY: How old is he now?

BERNIE: Going to be . . . six. Will you look at that?

DANNY: What?

BERNIE: They got a fucking fruit at the games counter. I
can't believe this. In the midst of the toy department. At the games counter, talking to the kids all
day long . . . a fairy.

DANNY: Yeah.

BERNIE: You know, one of those motherfuckers grabbed
me when I was Bobby's age.

DANNY: Where?

BERNIE: At the movies, where else? We're all wondering
what this old guy is doing at the cartoons, and he sits
down at the end of the row, and halfway through he
reaches over and grabs my joint. Reaches over *another* guy and grabs *me* by the joint.

DANNY: Was he rough?

BERNIE: What?

DANNY: I mean, was he rough about it?

BERNIE: Rough? *(Pause.)* I mean . . . *(Pause.)* Rough? What difference *how* he grabbed me? I mean, he's a *guy.*

DANNY: Yeah.

BERNIE: And *I'm* a guy. *(Pause.)* But at the time I was only a *kid,* for chrissakes. *(Pause.)*

DANNY: You ever do that stuff when you were kids?

BERNIE: What stuff?

DANNY: You know. Stuff with other kids.

BERNIE: Teasing? Like teasing the girls? Looking up their panties and so on?

DANNY: No, I mean when you were really young kids. Fooling around with the other kids . . . the other boys.

BERNIE: Fooling around? You mean like "messing" around with other boys?

DANNY: Fuck no. I didn't mean that. I just meant . . . you know.

BERNIE: *(Pause):* You mean fooling *around!* Sure, who didn't.

DANNY: Yeah.

BERNIE: Shit, we all used to fuck around.

DANNY: Right.

BERNIE: Even when we were little, shit. I mean you *learn* when you're young, right?

DANNY: Right.

BERNIE: And what you *learn*, that's what you *know*. Am I right?

DANNY: One Hundred Percent. It's all in your . . .

BERNIE: Head.

DANNY: . . . approach. *(Pause.)*

BERNIE: It's in your what?

DANNY: Approach?

BERNIE: Right.

DANNY: You know how to approach these things and you'll always be all right.

BERNIE: You don't learn right when you're young, those cocksuckers ruin your life.

DANNY: Who? *(Pause.)*

BERNIE: Anybody. *(Pause.)* Ruin it quicker'n you can turn around.

DANNY: Take you and that guy in the movies, for instance.

BERNIE: What do you mean?

DANNY: Just that if you'd been a little *older* . . .

BERNIE: Yeah?

DANNY: Or maybe the guy, if he'd been a little . . . younger . . .

BERNIE: What are you fucking talking about?

DANNY: I'm saying that if the circumstances . . .

BERNIE: What fucking circumstances? Some faggot queer got the hots for my joint at the cartoons.

DANNY: I'm not talking about *extenuating* circumstances, I only mean the circumstances of what happened.

BERNIE: And what exactly are you saying about them?

DANNY: All I'm saying . . .

BERNIE: . . . this happened *years* ago . . .

DANNY: . . . is that it could possibly have been damaging to you. *(Pause.)*

BERNIE: Yeah?

DANNY: . . . as a total Human Being.

BERNIE: Damn right.

DANNY: . . . and you're just lucky that it didn't.

BERNIE: Well, what the fuck, I was only a kid.

DANNY: Sure.

BERNIE: A kid laughs these things off. You forget, you go on living . . . what the fuck, huh?

DEB *and* JOAN's *apartment. Late at night. They are lounging.*

JOAN: Let's face it. He would prematurely ejaculate. There's no nicer way to say it. And the sooner he would come the guiltier he would feel and the sooner he would come. Because in some ways, of course, he was doing it to punish me. And he was doing a hell of a job of it.

So one day I said to him "Look, I'm in bed to make love with you, and you're in bed to make love with me. So why don't we just relax, and I'll be with you, and you be with me, and whenever you want to come is fine." *(Pause.)* But he still kept prematurely ejaculating. *(Pause.)* Although he did seem happier about it. *(Pause.)*

*Tableau.*

DEBORAH: We have any tuna fish?

JOAN: I think I ate it. *(Tableau.)*

*The Health Club.* BERNARD *in the gym talking to imaginary buddies.*

BERNIE: So the kid asks me "Bernie, blah, blah, blah, blah, blah, blah, blah, blah, blah, blah. The broad *this,* the broad *that,* blah blah blah." Right? So I tell him, "Dan, Dan, you think I don't know what you're feeling, I don't know what you're going through? You think about the broad, you *this,* you *that,* you think I don't know that?" So he tells me, "Bernie," he says, "I think I love her." *(Pause.)* Twenty-eight years old.

So I tell him, "Dan, Dan, I can *advise,* I can *counsel,* I can speak to you out of my *experience* . . . but in the final analysis, you are on your own. *(Pause.)* If you want my *opinion,* however, you are pussy-whipped." (I call 'em like I see 'em. I wouldn't say it if it wasn't so.) So what does he know at that age, huh? Sell his soul for a little eating pussy, and who can blame him. But mark my words: one, two more weeks, he'll do the right thing by the broad. *(Pause.)* And drop her like a fucking hot potato.

✵

JOAN *and* DEB *are out to lunch.*

JOAN: . . . and, of course, there exists the very real possibility that the whole thing is nothing other than a mistake of *rather* large magnitude, and that it never *was* supposed to work out.

DEBORAH: Do you really believe that?

JOAN: I don't know. I really don't know. I think I *do.* Well, look at your divorce rate. Look at the incidence of homosexuality . . . the number of violent, sex-connected crimes (this dressing is for shit) . . . all the antisocial behavior that chooses sex as its form of expression. Eh?

DEBORAH: I don't know.

JOAN: . . . physical and mental mutilations we perpetrate on each other, day in, day out . . . trying to fit ourselves to a pattern we can neither *understand* (although we pretend to) nor truly afford to *investigate* (although we pretend to). *(Pause.)* Come on, disagree with me.

DEBORAH: I disagree with you.

JOAN: It's a dirty joke, Deborah, the whole godforsaken business.

DEBORAH: I disagree with you.

JOAN: That's your right. Are you going to eat your roll? (DEB *shakes her head.*) Then perhaps *I* could have it. *(Takes roll.)* This roll is excellent.

DEBORAH: I'm moving in with Danny.

JOAN: I give you two months.

> DAN *and* BERNARD's *office.* DAN *is filing.* BERNARD *is talking on the phone.*

BERNIE: . . . so then she brings the dog in. "What's the pooch for?" I say. "Shut up and watch," she says. "You might learn something." . . . at the Laugh-Inn. *(Pause.)* They're open all night. *(Pause.)* No, they don't. *(Pause.)* I'm telling you they're open all night.

DANNY: They're open all night, Bern.

BERNIE *(to phone)*: I'm sorry. *(To* DAN*)* What?

DANNY: They're open all night.

BERNIE: Yeah. *(To phone)* They're open all night. *(Pause.)* A guy in the office. So then she gets down on the carpet with the dog . . .

DANNY: You want me to do these 11-13's?

BERNIE *(to* DAN*)*: Yeah. *(To phone)* So I'm just watching at this point. *(Pause.)* I'm getting to that. So the fucking dog, and may I be struck dead by lightning, his eyes light up, and he starts to grin. . . . *(Pause.)* . . . a fox terrier.

> DAN *and* DEB *are moving* DEB *out of her apartment.* JOAN *is in the background.*

DANNY: You have very interesting taste in music.

DEBORAH: A lot of them are Joan's.

DANNY: I'm sorry. . . . uh . . . *(To* JOAN) uh, which of these are yours? You want to separate them?

JOAN: Well, they aren't going to separate themselves, now, are they?

DANNY: No, I don't suppose they are. Why don't *you* separate them, Joan? *(Pause.)*

DEBORAH: Danny has a sauna in his building.

JOAN: How nice . . . sweating . . . Do you use your sauna often, Danny?

DANNY: I use the sauna from time to time. I'm fortunate in being blessed with the ability to sweat in the everyday course of events.

DEBORAH *(to* JOAN): What are we going to do about the television?

JOAN: Do you want to take it?

DANNY: I have a television.

JOAN: Let me just pay you for your half of it.

DEBORAH: You could send me a check.

JOAN: I could *give* you a check. You're not going to California for god's sake.

DEBORAH: I can pick it up next week.

JOAN: When?

DEBORAH: Whenever is convenient.

JOAN: Can you come by Tuesday night? . . . *(To* DAN) Can she come by Tuesday night?

DANNY: That's very good. That's very funny. Now could you find it in your heart to take the table lamp and shove it up your ass?

JOAN: Ah, that's very telling. On your instructions, I'm supposed to rend and torture myself anally. Is that what you like? Does Deborah know about this? You're moving out, move out.

DANNY: She's moving out. /

JOAN: Well, move *her* out, then and the hell with you. (*Pause. To* DEB) I hope you're very happy.

BERNARD *is at the office declaiming to some co-workers.*

BERNIE: Equal Rights Amendment? Equal Rights Amendment? I'll give you the fucking Equal Rights Amendment. Nobody ever wrote *me* no fucking amendments. Special *interest* groups, *okay* . . . but who's kidding who here, huh? (*Pause.*) We got baby seals dying in Alaska and we're writing amendments for *broads?* I mean, I'm a big fan of *society* . . . but this bites the big one. I'm sorry.

DAN *and* DEB's *apartment. The morning. They are each getting ready for work.*

DANNY: Do we have any shampoo?

DEBORAH: I don't know.

DANNY: You wash your hair at least twice a day. Shampoo is a staple item of your existence. Of course you know.

DEBORAH: All right. I *do*. Know.

DANNY: Do we have any shampoo?

DEBORAH: I don't know. Is your hair dirty?

DANNY: Does my hair look dirty?

DEBORAH: Does it feel dirty? *(Pause.)* It looks dirty.

DANNY: It feels greasy. I hate it when my hair feels greasy.

DEBORAH: Well, I'm not going to look. If you want to know if there's any shampoo, you go look for it.

DANNY: You don't have to look. You know very well if there's any shampoo or not. You're making me be ridiculous about this. *(Pause.)* You wash yourself too much anyway. If you really *used* all that shit they tell you in *Cosmopolitan* (and you do) you'd be washing yourself from morning till night. Pouring derivatives on yourself all day long.

DEBORAH: Will you love me when I'm old?

DANNY: If you can manage to look eighteen, yes.

DEBORAH: Now, that's very telling.

DANNY: You think so?

DEBORAH: Yes.

DANNY: I'm going to wash my hair. Is there any shampoo?

DEBORAH: Yes. And no.

DANNY: Now what's that supposed to mean?

DEBORAH: Everything. And nothing. *(Pause.)* Would you get my hose?

DANNY: No. Where does this come from? This whole fucking behavior. You're making it up. "Get my hose." You want your hose, I'll get your hose. Here's your fucking hose. *(Rummages in dresser.)* Where's your hose? *(Pause.)* What do they call them, anyway? Nobody says "hose."

DEBORAH: Pantyhose.

DANNY: Where are they?

DEBORAH: Get me some out of the laundry bag.

DANNY: You're going to wear dirty hose?

DEBORAH: I think I'm out of clean ones.

DANNY: So you're going downtown in dirty hose?

DEBORAH: Do you want me walking around with a naked la-la?

DANNY: If it makes you happy, Deb. I'm on the side of whatever makes you happy.

DEB *retrieves dirty hose from bag and starts changing into them.*

DANNY: You make me very horny.

DEBORAH: It's the idea of the dirty panties, Dan. You're sick.

DANNY: I love your breasts.

DEBORAH: "Thank you." *(Pause.)* Is that right?

DANNY: Fuck you.

DEBORAH: No hard feelings.

DANNY: Who said there were?

DEBORAH: You know there are.

DANNY: Then why say there aren't?

DAN's *office.* DAN *is talking to an imaginary co-worker.*

DANNY: . . no, wait a second. Wait a second. I want to tell you this. I know what you're saying, and I'm telling you I don't like you badmouthing the guy, who happens to be a friend of mine. So just let me tell my story, okay?

So the other day we're up on six and it's past five and I'm late, and I'm having some troubles with my chick (this chick I've been seeing) and I push the button and the elevator doesn't come, and it doesn't come, and it doesn't come, so I lean back and I kick the shit out of it three or four times (I was really hot). And *he,* he puts his arm around my shoulder and he calms me down and he says, "Dan, Dan . . . don't go looking for affection from inanimate objects." *(Pause.)* Huh? *(Pause.)* So I don't want to hear you badmouthing Bernie Litko.

DAN *and* DEB *in bed late at night.* DEB *is sleeping.*

DANNY: Deborah. Deb? Deb? You up?

*Pause.*

You sleeping?

*Pause.*

I can't sleep.

*Pause.*

You asleep?

*Pause.*

Huh?

*Pause.*

You sleeping, Deb?

*Pause.*

What are you thinking about?

*Pause.*

Deb?

*Pause.*

Did I wake you up?

*A movie theatre.* DAN *and* BERNARD *are watching a pornographic movie.*

BERNIE: Don't tell me that's that guy's joint. Whatever you do don't tell me that. That's not his joint. Tell me it's not his joint, Dan.

DANNY: It's his joint.

BERNIE: I don't want to hear it.

DANNY: That's what it is.

BERNIE: I don't want to hear it, so don't tell it to me. Nobody is hung like that. If that's his joint I'm going to go home and blow my brains out.

DANNY: He probably used a stand-in. *(Pause.)*

BERNIE: I can't stand this. I can't fucking stand this. *Lookit* that broad!

DANNY: Which one?

BERNIE: Which *one?* The one she looks a little bit like whatsername.

DANNY: Like Deborah?

BERNIE: Yeah.

DANNY: Which one is that?

BERNIE: That one.

DANNY: You think she looks like Deborah?

BERNIE: Yeah. You see what I mean?

DANNY: No. You think she's *pretty?*

BERNIE: Pretty? What the fuck are you talking about? *(Pause.)* You know this fucking house has changed.

DANNY: Yeah.

BERNIE: I mean, they still got the guys jerkin' off under the *Trib* in the front row . . .

DANNY: World's Greatest Newspaper.

BERNIE: . . . but they got a lot of scum in here now. Wait, now. Wait. Do you see that. Will you look at the fucking that?

DANNY: What?

BERNIE: That break in the action . . . they shifted scenes
. . . where they changed the camera angle . . . you
know why they do that? You know why? Because
the guy *came* is why, and they shift angles and wait
a while so it looks like he's fucking for hours. You see
that?

DANNY: Yeah.

BERNIE: These guys got no control. *(Pause.)* What was I
saying?

DANNY: How the house has changed.

BERNIE: They got a lot of scum in here now. DO YOU
SEE *THAT*? DO YOU FUCKING BELIEVE
THAT? *(Pause.)* A woman blowing a man's natural.
A woman blowing a dog's disgusting. *(Pause.)* Yeah,
that's what I think, and I'm not ashamed to say it!

DAN *and* DEB *at their apartment. In the midst of an
all-night argument.*

DEBORAH: Oh, shut up.

DANNY: I should shut up? Who's talking for the last
twelve hours straight, huh?

DEBORAH *motions him away in disgust.*

DANNY: . . . blah blah blah, blah blah blah, blah blah blah.
Jesus. Some people go home with the *Tribune.* You
go home with me. Everything's fine. Sex, talk, life,
everything. Until you want to get "closer," to get
"better." Do you know what the fuck you want?

Push. You push me.

Why can't you just see it for what it is?

DEBORAH: What?

DANNY: Us.

DEBORAH: And what is it?

DANNY: What it *is,* no more, no less.

DEBORAH: And what is that?

DANNY: Don't give me this. Don't give me that look, Missy.

DEBORAH: Or you're gonna what?

DANNY: I don't mind physical violence. I just can't stand emotional violence. *(Pause.)* I'm sorry. I'm sorry Deb. *(Pause.)* I forget who I'm talking to. I'm sorry. You're very good for me. Come here. *(Pause.)* Come here.

DEBORAH: No. You come here for christ's fucking sake. You want comfort, come get comfort. What am I, your toaster?

DANNY: Cunt.

DEBORAH: That's very good. "Cunt," good. Get it out. Let it all out.

DANNY: You cunt.

DEBORAH: We've established that.

DANNY: I try.

DEBORAH: You try and try. You are misunderstood and depressed.

DANNY: And you're no help.

DEBORAH: No, I'm a hindrance. You're trying to understand women and I'm confusing you with information. "Cunt" won't do it. "Fuck" won't do it. No more magic. What are you *feeling*. Tell me what you're *feeling*. Jerk.

DEB *alone.*

DEBORAH: My mother used to tell a story about how I came into the kitchen one day while she was preparing an important dish. I was about four. I said, "Mommy, can I have a cookie?", and she for some reason misunderstood or misheard me, and thought that I said that I wanted a "hug," so she gave me a "hug," and I said "Thank you, Mommy. I didn't want a cookie after all."

*(Pause.)* You see? What is a sublimation of what? *(Pause.)* What signifies what?

DAN *at* BERNARD's *apartment. The middle of the night. They are drunk.*

BERNIE: Tits and Ass. Tits and Ass. Tits and Ass. Tits and Ass. Blah de Bloo. Blah de Bloo. Blah de Bloo. Blah de Bloo. *(Pause.)* Huh?

DANNY: I don't know.

BERNIE: So *don't* know. Big deal—you are going to lose your head over a little bit of puss? You are going to sell your birthright for a mess of potash? "Oh, Bernie, she's *this*. Oh, Bernie, she's *that* . . ." You know what she is? She's a fucking human being just like you and me, Dan. We all have basically the same desires, and the shame of it is you get out of touch with yourself and lose your perspective. Huh?

*Pause.*

Huh?

*Pause.*

Yeah. You think you're playing with *kids? (Pause.)* Don't ever lose your sense of humor, Dan. Don't *ever* lose your sense of humor.

DAN *and* DEB *at their apartment. Splitting up their belongings.*

DANNY: . . . and your friend, Joan . . . that cunt was born in a carcrash. *(Pause.)* And your job is a lot of busywork, you know that?

DEBORAH: I know.

DANNY: And I have *no* fucking idea what your drawings mean. *(Pause.)* And you're a lousy fuck.

DEBORAH: I know.

DANNY: Your friend, *Joan,* is a better fuck than *you* are.

DEBORAH: I'm sure she is.

DANNY: . . . and *she's* a lousy fuck. *(Pause.)* Aren't you going to tell me I'm a lousy fuck?

DEBORAH: You *are* a lousy fuck.

DANNY: You're fulla shit.

DEB *and* JOAN *at their apartment.*

JOAN: You learn from your mistakes, Deborah. Man is the one animal who has that capacity.

DEBORAH: Yes.

JOAN: You can't live in the past.

DEBORAH: No.

JOAN: It does you no good.

DEBORAH: I know it.

JOAN: And, in the end, what do you have? You have your friends. *(Pause.)* Have you been drawing since you've been with Dan?

DEBORAH: It wasn't his fault.

JOAN: Well, whose fault was it, *mine?*

DEBORAH: It was my fault, Joan.

JOAN: It was not your fault. Say what you will, the *facts* don't change and the fact is if you take a grown man whose actions and whose outlook are those of a child, who wants nothing more or better than to have someone who will lick his penis and grin at his bizarre idea of wit, uh . . . if you take that man and uh . . .

DEBORAH: I'll thank you for this someday.

JOAN: Yes, you will, Deb. And you know, I truly don't see why you're being so hostile. I'm afraid I have to admit that.

JOAN *is reading a story to her imaginary toddlers.*

JOAN: . . . and when the Prince came home that night, she had changed into an old Hag (so of course he was very surprised).

"Where is my beautiful wife?" he asked the Hag. "And what have you done with her?"

And she said, "I am your wife." (That's right.)

"I can be beautiful during the daylight hours so that you and your friends can admire me, or I can be beautiful at night, so that you can enjoy me by the fireside, and so on. But for one half of the day I must be this old Hag you see before you."

*Pause.*

A "hag" is an ugly old lady.

*Pause.*

Well, how do you think it's spelled?

*Pause.*

Well, how does it sound?

*Pause.*

That's right. And so she told him . . .

DAN *and* BERNARD *are on the beach. They are looking at attractive women.*

BERNIE: Lookit this.

DANNY: Where?

BERNIE: *Lookit* this.

DANNY: Where?

BERNIE: There.

DANNY: *Oh* yeah.

BERNIE: My sweet goodness.

DANNY: Uh huh.

BERNIE: What a sensitive young lady.

DANNY: Check this one out.

BERNIE: Don't bother me.

DANNY: I'm telling you.

BERNIE: Where?

DANNY: Two o'clock.

BERNIE *(looks)*: Oh no!

DANNY: Yes.

BERNIE: Oh *no!*

DANNY: I'm afraid so.

BERNIE: I see no reason to go on living.

DANNY: Ummm.

BERNIE: There can be no more to life.

DANNY: Yes.

BERNIE: In a way it's sad. To think I gaze upon the highest man can wish for . . .

DANNY: Bernie . . .

BERNIE: His destiny . . .

DANNY: Bernie . . .

BERNIE: The fruition of a pain-laden stay on earth . . .

DANNY: Hey, Bernie, isn't that whatsername?

BERNIE: Her?

DANNY: Yeah.

BERNIE: Is she who?

DANNY: *Whatz*ername, who you introduced me to last week.

BERNIE: Naaa. This broad is much better looking.

DANNY: I think it's her.

BERNIE: This broad has a lot more class.

DANNY: No . . .

BERNIE: Lookit her boobs. *(Pause.)* Am I right or not?

DANNY: Yeah, I think you're right.

BERNIE: Hey! Don't look behind you.

DANNY: Yeah?

BERNIE: Whatever you do, don't look behind you.

DANNY: Where?

BERNIE: Right behind you, about ten feet behind you to your right.

DANNY: Yeah?

BERNIE: I'm telling you.

DANNY *(looks)*: Get the fuck *outta* here!

BERNIE: Can I pick 'em?

DANNY: Bernie . . .

BERNIE: Is the radar in fine shape?

DANNY: . . . I gotta say . . .

BERNIE: . . . *Oh* yeah . . .

DANNY: . . . that you can *pick* 'em.

BERNIE: I know I can. And will you look at the chick in the two piece wet-look jobbie?

DANNY: Where?

BERNIE: Where I'm looking. *(Pause.)* Those *legs* . . .

DANNY: Oh *no!*

BERNIE: . . . all the way up to her *ass!*

DANNY: Jesus.

BERNIE: And *beyond* for all we know.

DANNY: You said it.

BERNIE: *Look*it her.

DANNY: Yup.

BERNIE: Fuckin' *look*it her.

DANNY: I know it.

BERNIE: Tell me she is not flaunting herself all over the beach.

DANNY: She is casting it to the winds.

BERNIE: Look at that *suit.*

DANNY: Bern . . . Bernie . . . I think that I can see her snatch.

BERNIE: You're fulla shit.

DANNY: On my honor. I can see her fucking snatch.

BERNIE: You can see her snatch?

DANNY: I'm telling you.

BERNIE *(looks)*: I can't make it out.

DANNY: At the top of her legs.

BERNIE: I know where it is, I just can't see it.

DANNY: When she breathes in. You gotta look close.

*Pause. They look.*

BERNIE: Where does she get off with that noise?

DANNY: Yeah.

BERNIE: That fuckin' pisses me off.

DANNY: Yeah.

BERNIE: That pisses the *fuck* off outta me.

DANNY: I know.

BERNIE: Piss.

DANNY: Cockteaser.

BERNIE: Prissy little cunt.

DANNY: Right on the beach.

BERNIE: Piss me off.

DANNY: Little prude.

BERNIE: On the fucking beach.

DANNY: And those *tits!*

BERNIE: Don't talk to me about tits.

DANNY: Nice firm tits.

BERNIE: Where does she get off with those tits?

DANNY: What a pair of boobs.

BERNIE: Not that I'm a tit man . . .

DANNY: I know.

BERNIE: I mean, I *dig* tits . . .

DANNY: I don't blame you.

BERNIE: . . . but I wouldn't go out of my way for a pair of tits.

DANNY: Yeah.

BERNIE: The way I see it, *tits* . . .

DANNY: Yeah?

BERNIE: . . . are what you make of 'em.

DANNY: It's like anything else.

BERNIE: But an *ass* . . .

DANNY: Yeah.

BERNIE: . . . is an *ass*.

DANNY: Goes without saying. You know what I like?

BERNIE: What?

DANNY: Stomach muscles.

BERNIE: You're talking about flab.

DANNY: Yeah.

BERNIE: I know what you're talking about.

DANNY: I know you do.

BERNIE: Flab.

DANNY: Fuckin' flab.

BERNIE: Who needs it?

DANNY: More trouble than it's worth.

BERNIE: A nice pair of legs though . . .

DANNY: I know it.

BERNIE: . . . is like money from home.

DANNY: A home *away* from home.

BERNIE: Now look over there to illustrate my point.

DANNY: The broad?

BERNIE: Right. Nice legs, eh?

DANNY: Yup.

BERNIE: Very acceptable old ass . . .

DANNY: Nice, firm.

BERNIE: Flat belly, beautiful pair of tits.

DANNY: No question.

BERNIE: Now *she* is fine. *(Pause.)*

DANNY: Right.

BERNIE: But now look over *there*. The broad with the dumpy legs and the fat whatdayacallit.

DANNY: Stomach.

BERNIE: Her legs are for shit, her stomach is dumpy, her

tits don't say anything for her, and her muscle tone is not good.

DANNY: Right.

BERNIE: Now she is *not* a good-looking girl. *(Pause.)* In fact she is something of a pig. *(Pause.)* You see? That's all it takes . . . to make the difference between a knockout looking broad, and a nothing look-ing broad who doesn't look like anything. *(Pause.)* You see my point?

DANNY: . . . yeah?

BERNIE: Makes all the fucking difference in the world. *(Pause.)* Coming out here on the beach. Lying all over the beach, flaunting their bodies . . . I mean who the fuck do they think they are all of a sudden, coming out here and just flaunting their bodies all over? *(Pause.)* I mean, what are you supposed to think? I come to the beach with a friend to get some sun and watch the action and . . . I mean a fellow comes to the beach to sit out in the fucking sun, am I wrong? . . . I mean we're talking about recreational fucking space, huh? . . . huh? *(Pause.)* What the fuck am I talking about?

DANNY: Are you feeling all right?

BERNIE: Well, how do I look, do I look all right?

DANNY: Sure.

BERNIE: Well, then let's assume that I feel all right, okay?

DANNY: Okay.

BERNIE: I mean, how could you feel anything *but* all right, for chrissakes? Will you look at that body?

*(Pause.)* What a pair of tits. *(Pause.)* With tits like that, who needs . . . anything.

*A long pause. They watch an imaginary woman pass in front of them.*

BERNIE: Hi.

DANNY: Hello there.

*Pause. She walks by.*

BERNIE: She's probably deaf.

DANNY: She did *look* deaf, didn't she.

BERNIE: Yeah. *(Pause.)*

DANNY: Deaf *bitch*.

# The Duck
# Variations

*The Duck Variations* was first produced by The St. Nicholas Theater Company, at Goddard College, Plainfield, Vermont, in 1972, with the following cast:

| | |
|---|---|
| EMIL VARĚC | Pablo Vela |
| GEORGE S. ARONOVITZ | Peter Vincent |

It was directed by David Mamet; set and lighting by Jim Drake.

It was first produced off-off Broadway at St. Clements Theatre, New York City, in 1975, with the following cast:

| | |
|---|---|
| EMIL VARĚC | Paul Sparer |
| GEORGE S. ARONOVITZ | Michael Egan |

It was directed by Albert Takazauckas; set by Michael Massee; lighting by Gary Porto.

It was produced off-Broadway at the Cherry Lane Theatre, New York City, with *Sexual Perversity in Chicago*, in June of 1976, with the following cast:

| | |
|---|---|
| EMIL VARĚC | Mike Kellin |
| GEORGE S. ARONOVITZ | Michael Egan |

It was directed by Albert Takazauckas; set by Michael Massee; lighting by Gary Porto.

# The Scene:

A Park on the edge of a Big City on a Lake.
An afternoon around Easter.

# The Characters:

Emil Varĕc and George S. Aronovitz. Two
gentlemen in their sixties.

This is a very simple play.

The set should consist only of a park bench and
perhaps a wire garbage can.

The actors can be discovered seated on the
bench at rise, or they can come on together, or
separately and meet.

Any blocking or business is at the discretion of
individual actors and directors.

There should be, though, an interval between
each variation—it doesn't need to be a long one—
to allow the actors to rest and prepare for the
new variation. This interval is analogous to the
space between movements in a musical presen-
tation.

# The Duck Variations

# "It's Nice, The Park Is Nice"

EMIL:   It's Nice.

GEORGE:   The Park is nice.

EMIL:   You forget.

GEORGE:   . . . you remember.

EMIL:   I don't know . . .

GEORGE:   What's to know? There's a boat!

EMIL:   So early?

GEORGE:   I suppose so. . . . because there it is.

EMIL:   I wonder if it's cold out there.

GEORGE:   There, here, it's like it is today. How it is *today*, that's how it is.

EMIL:   But the boat is moving . . .

GEORGE:   So it's colder in relation how fast the boat is going.

EMIL:   The water is colder than the land.

GEORGE:   So it's cold in relation to the water.

EMIL:   So it's a different temperature on the boat than on a bench.

GEORGE:   They probably got sweaters.

EMIL: There's more than one in the boat?

GEORGE: Wait till they come round again.

EMIL: Where did they go?

GEORGE: Over there, behind the pier, where could they go?

EMIL: Not far . . . it's expensive a boat.

GEORGE: They care?

EMIL: No.

GEORGE: If they got the money for a *boat*, they can afford it.

EMIL: It's not cheap.

GEORGE: I said it was cheap?

EMIL: Even a small boat.

GEORGE: I know it's not cheap.

EMIL: Even a very small boat is expensive.

GEORGE: Many times a small boat is even *more* expensive.

EMIL: Ah.

GEORGE: Depending . . .

EMIL: Mmm.

GEORGE: On many factors.

EMIL: Mmm.

GEORGE: . . . the size of the boat . . .

EMIL: Yes.

GEORGE: . . . the engine.

EMIL: Yes. The *size* of the engine.

GEORGE: Certainly, certainly.

EMIL: The speed of the engine.

GEORGE: Many factors.

EMIL: The speed of the *boat.*

GEORGE: That. None of it's cheap. It's all very intricate.

EMIL: Cars.

GEORGE: Boats, cars . . . air travel. The military. It was never cheap.

EMIL: Housing.

GEORGE (*looks*): There's two of them in the boat.

EMIL: It's the same boat?

GEORGE: How many boats have we seen today?

EMIL: That's what I'm asking.

GEORGE: One.

EMIL (*looks*): Another boat!

GEORGE: One, two . . .

EMIL: A real clipper, too.

GEORGE: Where?

EMIL: Look at *her* will ya!

GEORGE: That?

EMIL: What else? Go, sister!

GEORGE:  That?

EMIL:  Sure as shootin'.

GEORGE:  That's the water pump.

EMIL:  That?

GEORGE:  Yes.

EMIL:  That?

GEORGE:  Yes.

EMIL:  The pump house?

GEORGE:  Yes.

EMIL:  She's the water pump?

GEORGE:  Yes.

EMIL:  . . . look at her float.

GEORGE:  Mmm.

EMIL:  Look at her . . . just sit there.

GEORGE:  Mmm.

EMIL:  All year 'round.

GEORGE:  I'll give you that.

EMIL:  What a life.

GEORGE:  Ducks!

EMIL:  Where?

GEORGE:  Where I'm pointing.

EMIL:  Ahh.

GEORGE:  A sure sign of spring.

EMIL:    Autumn, too.

GEORGE:    Uh huh.

EMIL:    . . . you see them . . .

GEORGE:    Yes.

EMIL:    They go south . . .

GEORGE:    Um.

EMIL:    They come back . . .

GEORGE:    Ummm.

EMIL:    They live . . .

GEORGE:    They go . . .

EMIL:    Ahhh.

GEORGE:    Ducks like to go . . .

EMIL:    . . . yes?

GEORGE:    Where it's *nice* . . .

EMIL:    Ehhh?

GEORGE:    *At that time!*

EMIL:    Of course.

GEORGE:    And they're made so they just go. Something inside says it's getting a little cold . . . a little too cold . . .

EMIL:    Like humans, they don't like cold.

GEORGE:    And there they go.

EMIL:    There they go.

GEORGE:    And the same when it's warm.

EMIL:   They come back.

GEORGE: They got a leader. A lead duck. He starts . . .
        he's a duck. But he stays with the pack. Many
        times. He comes, he goes. He learns the route.
        Maybe he's got a little more on the ball.

EMIL:   All this time there is another lead duck.

GEORGE: Of course. But *He*, he goes, he lives, maybe he
        finds a mate . . .

EMIL:   Yes.

GEORGE: And he *waits*. . . . The *lead* duck . . . who
        knows?

EMIL:   He dies.

GEORGE: One day, yes. He dies. He gets lost . . .

EMIL:   And our duck moves up.

GEORGE: *He* is now the leader. It is *he* who guides them
        from one home to the next. They all know the
        way. Each of them has it in him to know when
        the time is to move. . . . But *he* . . . He will be in
        charge until . . .

EMIL:   Yes.

GEORGE: Just like the other one . . .

EMIL:   There's no shame in that.

GEORGE: Just like the previous duck . . .

EMIL:   It happened to *him*, it's got to happen to *him*.

GEORGE: The time comes to step down.

EMIL:   He dies.

GEORGE: He dies, he leaves . . . something. And another duck moves on up.

EMIL: And *someday*.

GEORGE: Yes.

EMIL: Someone will take *his* place.

GEORGE: Until . . .

EMIL: It's boring just to think about it.

## SECOND VARIATION
# "The Duck's Life"

GEORGE: You know, the duck's life is not all hearts and flowers. He's got his worries, too. He's got fleas and lice and diseases of the body. Delusions. Wing problems. Sexual difficulties. Many things.

EMIL: It's not an easy life.

GEORGE: Only the beginning. The duck is at the mercy of any elements in the vicinity. Sunspots. Miscarriage. Inappropriate changes in the weather.

EMIL: Yes.

GEORGE: Hunters. Blight. Tornadoes. Traps. Any number of airplanes.

EMIL: Small vicious children.

GEORGE: Chainstores. And, of course, the Blue Heron.

EMIL: Blue Heron?

GEORGE: The hereditary Enemy of the Duck.

EMIL: Yeah?

GEORGE: It's what they call symbiosis. They both live to insure the happiness of each other. The Blue Herons eat ducks, and the duck . . .

EMIL: Yes?

GEORGE: The duck's part of the bargain . . .

EMIL: Is to be eaten by the Heron?

GEORGE: Is to . . . Well it slips me for the moment, but it's not as one-sided as it might appear. Nature has given the duck speed and endurance and the art of concealment. She has made the Heron large and unwieldy and *blue* to be able to spot at a distance. On the other hand he has the benefits of size and occasional camouflage should he come up against something blue.

EMIL: And shaped like a bird.

GEORGE: Not always necessary. The battle between the two is as old as time. The ducks propagating, the Herons eating them. The Herons multiplying and losing great numbers to exhaustion in the never-ending chase of the duck. Each keeping the other in check, down through history, until a bond of unspoken friendship and respect unites them, even in the embrace of death.

EMIL: So why do they continue to fight?

GEORGE: Survival of the fittest. The never-ending struggle between heredity and environment. The urge to combat. Old as the oceans. Instilled in us all. Who can say to what purpose?

EMIL: Who?

GEORGE: We do not know. But this much we *do* know. As long as the duck exists, he will battle day and night, sick and well with the Heron, for so is it writ. And as long as the sky is made dark with the wing of the Monster Bird, the Heron will feast on duck.

# "Also They Got Barnyard Ducks"

EMIL: Also they got barnyard ducks.

GEORGE: Yeah. I know.

EMIL: That they raise for Easter and Thanksgiving.

GEORGE: You're thinking of Turkeys.

EMIL: Also ducks.

GEORGE: They keep 'em? In captivity?

EMIL: Yeah. In the Barnyard. They clip their wings.

GEORGE: Uh.

EMIL: Yeah. What? You can't put 'em on their honor?!

GEORGE: Times have changed.

EMIL: Vandalism . . . . . . they fat 'em up. They feed 'em, the farmers, on special mixtures. Corn, and maybe an oat. And they got special injections they give 'em. To keep 'em happy.

GEORGE: And they can't fly.

EMIL: No.

GEORGE: All with wildness is gone.

EMIL: Just walking around the farm all day. Eating.

GEORGE: They're allowed to mate?

EMIL:    This we do not know.

GEORGE:  Eh?

EMIL:    Only a few farmers know this.

GEORGE:  Yeah?

EMIL:    The mating of ducks is a private matter between the duck in question and his mate.

GEORGE:  Yeah?

EMIL:    It is a thing which few White men have witnessed. . . . And those who claim to have seen it . . . strangely do not wish to speak.

GEORGE:  There are things we're better off not to know.

EMIL:    If you don't know, you never can be forced to tell.

GEORGE:  They don't got those beaks for nothing.

EMIL:    *Nothing* is for Nothing.

GEORGE:  Too true.

EMIL:    Everything has got a purpose.

GEORGE:  True. . . .

EMIL:    Every blessed thing . . .

GEORGE:  Oh yes.

EMIL:    . . . that lives has got a purpose.

GEORGE:  Ducks . . .

EMIL:    Sweat glands . . .

GEORGE:  Yeah.

EMIL:    We don't sweat for nothing, you know.

GEORGE: I know it.

EMIL: Everything that lives must sweat.

GEORGE: It's all got a purpose.

EMIL: It's all got a rhyme *and* a reason.

GEORGE: The purpose of sweat is, in itself, not clear.

EMIL: Yes . . .

GEORGE: But . . . there it is.

EMIL: A purpose and a reason. Even those we, at this time, do not clearly understand.

GEORGE: Sure as shootin'.

EMIL: The yearly migration of the duck, to mate and take a little rest . . .

GEORGE: Purpose.

EMIL: Sweat . . .

GEORGE: Purpose.

EMIL: There's nothing you could possibly name that doesn't have a purpose. Don't even bother to try. Don't waste your time.

GEORGE: I'm in no hurry.

EMIL: It's all got a purpose. The very fact that you are sitting here right now on this bench has got a purpose.

GEORGE: And so, by process of elimination, does the bench.

EMIL: Now you're talking sense.

GEORGE: Darn Tootin'.

EMIL: The law of the universe is a law unto itself.

GEORGE: Yes. Yes.

EMIL: And woe be to the man who fools around.

GEORGE: You can't get away with *nothing*.

EMIL: And if you *could* it would have a purpose.

GEORGE: Nobody knows that better than me.

EMIL: . . . Well put.

# "The Duck Is Not Like Us"

EMIL:    The duck is not like us, you know.

GEORGE:  How so?

EMIL:    The Duck is an egg-bearing creature.

GEORGE:  And we're not, I suppose?

EMIL:    I didn't say that. The young of the duck at birth are already trained to do things most humans learn only much later. Swim. Follow their mother.

GEORGE:  Fly.

EMIL:    No. I don't believe they can fly until later life.

GEORGE:  But it's possible.

EMIL:    It's possible, but you're wrong.

GEORGE:  . . . As a matter of fact I do remember reading somewhere that many small ducks *do* possess the ability to fly at birth.

EMIL:    I do think you are mistaken.

GEORGE:  No. It could be. . . . But no.

EMIL:    Yes. I believe you're sadly wrong.

GEORGE:  No. I wouldn't *swear* to it. . . .

EMIL: No.

GEORGE: But I'd almost *swear* I've read that *some-where.* . . .

EMIL: Yes, I'm fairly sure you're wrong on that one point.

GEORGE: Some little-known group of ducks.

EMIL: No. All my knowledge of nature tells me I must say no.

GEORGE: A very small group of ducks.

EMIL: I can not let that by.

GEORGE: But I think . . .

EMIL: It's possible you *misread* the . . .

GEORGE: Possibly, but . . .

EMIL: No, no. No. I must still stick to my saying no. No.

GEORGE: . . . Perhaps I misread it. What a thing, how-ever. To be able to fly. In later life.

EMIL: Swimming ain't so bad either.

GEORGE: But any fool who knows how to swim can swim. It takes a *bird* to Fly.

EMIL: Insects also fly.

GEORGE: But not in the same category.

EMIL: Insects . . . birds and insects and . . . I *could* be wrong but . . .

GEORGE: You *are* wrong. Nothing else flies.

# "Did You Know What I Was Reading"

GEORGE: Did you know what I was reading Somewhere?

EMIL: Don't start.

GEORGE: About the Stratosphere. The Stratosphere, particularly the lower stratosphere, is becoming messy with gook.

EMIL: Eh?

GEORGE: According to the weatherman.

EMIL: *Our* Stratosphere?

GEORGE: Everybody's. Because it's all the same thing.

EMIL: Eh?

GEORGE: As if you drop a pebble in a pond and the ripples spread you-know-not-where . . .

EMIL: Yes?

GEORGE: So, when you stick shit up in the Stratosphere . . .

EMIL: Yes?

GEORGE: You got the same problem.

EMIL: What kind of gook?

GEORGE: All kinds. Dirt . . .

EMIL: Yes.

GEORGE: Gook . . .

EMIL: No good.

GEORGE: Automotive . . .

EMIL: Yeah.

GEORGE: Cigarette smoke. It's all up there. It's not going anywhere.

EMIL: Yeah.

GEORGE: They're finding out many things about the world we live in from the air.

EMIL: Yes.

GEORGE: For, in Many ways . . . the air is more a part of our world than we would like to admit. Think about it.

EMIL: I will.

GEORGE: Planes that come down, they got to wash 'em right away. They go up clean, they come down filthy.

EMIL: Yes.

GEORGE: But the creatures with no choice: Insects, ducks.

EMIL: Gliders.

GEORGE: It's a shame. They should be shot.

EMIL: Some of them are shot.

GEORGE: No, *them,* the ones responsible. Ducks! They're finding ducks with lung cancer. I was reading about this hunter in the forest and he shot a bunch of ducks that were laying down . . .

EMIL: Yes.

GEORGE: And he missed. *But!* As he was walking away he heard this hacking, and he went back to investigate. And there were these five or six stunted ducks sitting in a clearing, hacking their guts out.

EMIL: No!

GEORGE: Coughing and sneezing. Runny noses . . . and they'd flap their wings and go maybe two flaps and fall down coughing.

EMIL: It's no good for you.

GEORGE: And he says instead of running off they all came up and huddled around his feet with these rheumy, runny eyes. Looking quite pathetic. And he says he couldn't get it out of his mind. . . .

EMIL: What?

GEORGE: I'll feel silly to say it.

EMIL: Tell me.

GEORGE: That they looked like they were trying to bum a smoke.

EMIL: . . . That's ridiculous.

GEORGE: I know it.

EMIL: I think someone is putting you on.

GEORGE: Very likely.

EMIL: You aren't even *supposed* to smoke in a forest.

GEORGE: Go fight City Hall.

# "What Kind Of A World Is It"

GEORGE: What kind of a world is it that can't even keep
its streets clean?

EMIL: A self-destructive world.

GEORGE: You said it.

EMIL: A cruel world.

GEORGE: A dirty world. Feh. I'm getting old.

EMIL: Nobody's getting any younger.

GEORGE: Almost makes a feller want to stop trying.

EMIL: Stop trying what?

GEORGE: You know, life is a lot simpler than many people would like us to believe.

EMIL: How so?

GEORGE: Take the duck.

EMIL: All right.

GEORGE: Of what does his life consist?

EMIL: Well, flying . . .

GEORGE: Yes.

EMIL: Eating.

GEORGE: Yes.

EMIL: Sleeping.

GEORGE: Yes.

EMIL: Washing himself.

GEORGE: Yes.

EMIL: Mating.

GEORGE: Yes.

EMIL: And perhaps getting himself shot by some jerk in a red hat.

GEORGE: Or "Death."

EMIL: Should we include that as one of the activities of life?

GEORGE: Well, you can't die in a vacuum.

EMIL: That's true.

GEORGE: So there we have it: the duck, too, is doomed to death . . .

EMIL: As are we all.

GEORGE: But his life prior to that point is so much more simple. He is born. He learns his trade: to fly. He flies, he eats, he finds a mate, he has young, he flies some more, he dies. A simple, straightforward easy-to-handle life.

EMIL: So what's your point?

GEORGE: Well, lookit:

EMIL: Okay.

GEORGE: On his deathbed what does the duck say if only he could speak?

EMIL: He wants to live some more.

GEORGE: Right. But remorse? Guilt? Other bad feelings? No. No. He is in tune with nature.

EMIL: He is a part of nature. He is a duck.

GEORGE: Yes, but so is man a part of nature.

EMIL: Speak for yourself.

GEORGE: I am speaking for myself.

EMIL: Then speak to yourself.

GEORGE: Who asked you to listen?

EMIL: Who asked you to talk?

GEORGE: Why are you getting upset?

EMIL: You upset me.

GEORGE: Yeah?

EMIL: With your talk of nature and the duck and death. Morbid useless talk. You know, it is a good thing to be perceptive, but you shouldn't let it get in the way.

GEORGE: And that is the point I was trying to make.

## SEVENTH VARIATION
# "Yes, In Many Ways"

GEORGE: Yes, in many ways Nature is our window to the world.

EMIL: Nature *is* the world.

GEORGE: Which shows you how easy it is to take a good idea and glop it up.

EMIL: So who do you complain to.

GEORGE: Well, you complain to me.

EMIL: Do you mind?

GEORGE: I'm glad I got the time to listen.

EMIL: A man needs a friend in this life.

GEORGE: In this or any other life.

EMIL: You said it. Without a friend, life is not . . .

GEORGE: Worth living?

EMIL: No it's still worth living. I mean, what is worth living if not life? No. But life without a friend is . . .

GEORGE: It's lonely.

EMIL: It sure is. You said it. It's good to have a friend.

GEORGE: It's good to be a friend.

EMIL: It's good to have a friend to talk to.

GEORGE: It's good to talk to a friend.

EMIL: To complain to a friend . . .

GEORGE: It's good to listen . . .

EMIL: Is good.

GEORGE: To a friend.

EMIL: To make life a little less full of pain . . .

GEORGE: I'd try anything.

EMIL: Is good.

GEORGE: For you, or for a friend. Because it's good to help.

EMIL: To help a friend in need is the most that any man can want to do.

GEORGE: And you couldn't ask for more than that.

EMIL: I wouldn't.

GEORGE: Good.

EMIL: Being a loner in this world . . .

GEORGE: Is not my bag of tea.

EMIL: Is no good. No man is an Island to himself.

GEORGE: Or to anyone else.

EMIL: You can't live alone forever. You can't live forever anyway. But you can't live alone. Nothing that lives can live alone. Flowers. You never find just one flower. Trees. Ducks.

GEORGE: Cactus.

EMIL: Lives alone?

GEORGE: Well, you take the cactus in the waste. It stands alone as far as the eye can tell.

EMIL: But there are other cacti.

GEORGE: Not in that immediate area, no.

EMIL: What are you trying to say?

GEORGE: That the *cactus,* unlike everything else that cannot live alone, *thrives* . . .

EMIL: I don't want to hear it.

GEORGE: But it's true, the cactus.

EMIL: I don't want to hear it. If it's false, don't waste my time and if it is true I don't want to know.

GEORGE: It's a proven fact.

EMIL: I can't hear you.

GEORGE: Even the duck sometimes.

EMIL *(looks)*: . . . Nothing that lives can live alone.

# "Ahh, I Don't Know"

EMIL:    Ahh, I don't know.

GEORGE:  So what?

EMIL:    You gotta point. . . . Sometimes I think the Park is more trouble than it's worth.

GEORGE:  How so?

EMIL:    To come and look at the Lake and the Trees and Animals and Sun just once in a while and traipse back. Back to . . .

GEORGE:  Your apartment.

EMIL:    Joyless. Cold concrete. Apartment. Stuff. Linoleum. Imitation.

GEORGE:  The park is more real?

EMIL:    The Park? Yes.

GEORGE:  Sitting on benches.

EMIL:    Yes.

GEORGE:  Visiting tame animals?

EMIL:    Taken from wildest captivity.

GEORGE:  Watching a lake that's a sewer?

EMIL:    At least it's water.

GEORGE: You wanna drink it?

EMIL: I drink it every day.

GEORGE: Yeah. After it's been pured and filtered.

EMIL: A lake just the same. My Inland Sea.

GEORGE: Fulla Inland Shit.

EMIL: It's better than nothing.

GEORGE: Nothing is better than nothing.

EMIL: Well, it's a close second.

GEORGE: But why does it hurt you to come to the park?

EMIL: I sit Home, I can come to the park. At the park the only place I have to go is home.

GEORGE: Better not to have a park?

EMIL: I don't know.

GEORGE: Better not to have a Zoo? We should forget what a turtle is?

EMIL: Aaaaah.

GEORGE: Our Children should never know the joy of watching some animal . . . behaving?

EMIL: I don't know.

GEORGE: They should stay home and know only guppies eating their young.

EMIL: Let 'em go to the Country. Nature's play-ground.
The Country.
The Land that Time Forgot.
Mallards in Formation.

Individual barnyard noises.
Horses.
Rusty Gates.
An ancient tractor.
Hay, barley.
Mushrooms.
Rye.
Stuffed full of abundance.
Enough to feed the nations of the World.

GEORGE: We'll have 'em over. We don't get enough riff-raff.

EMIL: Enough to gorge the countless cows of South America.

GEORGE: Did you make that up?

EMIL: Yes.

GEORGE: I take my hat off to you.

EMIL: Thank you.

GEORGE: "Feed the many" . . . how does it go?

EMIL: Um. Stuff the nameless . . . It'll come to me.

GEORGE: When you get it, tell me.

## NINTH VARIATION
# "At The Zoo They Got Ducks"

EMIL: At the Zoo they got ducks. They got. What do you call it? . . . A Mallard. They got a mallard and a . . . what is it? A cantaloupe.

GEORGE: You mean an antelope.

EMIL: No . . . no, it's not cantaloupe. But it's *like* cantaloupe. Uh . . .

GEORGE: Antelope?

EMIL: No! *Antelope* is like an elk. What *I'm* thinking is like a duck.

GEORGE: Goose?

EMIL: No. But it's . . . What sounds like *cantaloupe,* but it isn't.

GEORGE: . . . Antelope. I'm sorry, but that's it.

EMIL: No. Wait! Wait. Ca . . . cala . . . camma . . . grantal . . .

GEORGE: Canadian ducks?

EMIL: No! I've *seen* 'em, the ones I mean. I've seen 'em in the Zoo.

GEORGE: Ducks?

EMIL: Yes! Ducks that I'm talking about. By God, I know what I mean . . . They're called . . . The

only thing that comes up is canta. Pantel. Pan-
del. Panda . . . Candarolpe . . .

GEORGE: They ain't got no panda.

EMIL: I know it . . . Panna . . .

GEORGE: They *had* a panda at the *other* Zoo but it died.

EMIL: Yeah. Nanna . . .

GEORGE: There were two of 'em. Or three. But they were
all men and when they died . . . they couldn't
have any babies, of course . . .

EMIL: Randspan?

GEORGE: . . . so the Pandas . . .

EMIL: . . . lope . . .

GEORGE: Died.

EMIL: Lo . . . lopa? Loola . . .

GEORGE: Not Swans?

EMIL: No. Please. I know Swans. I'm talking about
ducks.

GEORGE: I know it.

EMIL: Can . . .

GEORGE: Those Pandas were something.

EMIL: Yeah.

GEORGE: Giant Pandas.

EMIL: Yeah.

GEORGE: *Big* things.

EMIL: I've seen 'em.

GEORGE: Not lately you haven't.

EMIL: No.

GEORGE: Cause they been dead.

EMIL: I know it.

GEORGE: From the Orient. Pandas from the Far East. There for all to see.

EMIL: Mantalope?

GEORGE: Black and White.

EMIL: Palapope . . .

GEORGE: Together.

EMIL: Maaaa . . .

GEORGE: The Giant Panda.

EMIL: Fanna . . .

GEORGE: Over two stories tall.

EMIL: Raaa?

GEORGE: It got too expensive to feed it. They had to put 'em to sleep.

# "It's A Crying Shame"

EMIL: It's a crying shame.

GEORGE: Eh?

EMIL: A crying piss-laden shame. A blot on our time. Gook on the scutcheon. Oil slicks from here to Africa.

GEORGE: Huh?

EMIL: They don't allow no smoking on ocean liners. One spark overboard and the whole ocean goes.

GEORGE: Yeah?

EMIL: Oil-bearing ducks floating up dead on the beaches. Beaches closing. No place to swim. The surface of the sea is solid dying wildlife. In Australia . . . they're finding fish, they're going blind from lack of sun. New scary species are developing. They eat nothing but dead birds.

GEORGE: Yeah?

EMIL: Catfish.

GEORGE: . . . I think that's something different.

EMIL: Nevermore. Thrushes. No more the duck. Bluejays. Cardinals. Making the dead ocean their last home.

GEORGE: When I was young . . .

EMIL: Floating up dead on the beaches.

GEORGE: Around my house . . .

EMIL: Their lungs a sodden pulp of gasoline. They're made for something better than that.

GEORGE: In the springtime we used to . . .

EMIL: Can't even burn leaves in the fall. We have to wrap them in Plastic. Next we'll have to wrap each leaf individually. Little envelopes for each leaf, it shouldn't contaminate us with the vapors. Little numbered packets.

GEORGE: Our lawn was.

EMIL: What?

GEORGE: Eh?

EMIL: What was your lawn?

GEORGE: I forget.

EMIL: Can you imagine, being the last man alive to have seen a blue heron? Or a wild buffalo?

GEORGE: No man can live in the path of a wild buffalo.

EMIL: All right. A regular buffalo, then.

GEORGE: They got 'em at the zoo.

EMIL: Buffaloes?

GEORGE: Yeah, they got plenty of 'em.

EMIL:    But that's in captivity.

GEORGE:  I should hope so.

EMIL:    Well, in any case, you see my point.

GEORGE:  Yes . . .

EMIL:    Well, that's the point I was trying to make.

# "You Know, I Remember"

GEORGE: You know, I remember reading somewhere . . .

EMIL: Please.

GEORGE: All right.

EMIL: I hurt your feelings.

GEORGE: Yes.

EMIL: I'm sorry.

GEORGE: I know.

EMIL: There is no excuse for that.

GEORGE: It's all right.

EMIL: What were you gonna say?

GEORGE: About the balance of nature.

EMIL: Yes?

GEORGE: Being dependent on one of the Professional Spectator Sports.

EMIL: You're fulla shit.

GEORGE: For its continuation.

EMIL: What made you think of that?

GEORGE: I'm not sure.

EMIL:    Some sport?

GEORGE:  I don't know.

EMIL:    Nature?

GEORGE:  Perhaps.

EMIL:    Do you remember which sport?

GEORGE:  I . . . no, I wouldn't want to go on record as remembering. One of the Major League sports.

EMIL:    Where did you read it?

GEORGE:  I don't know. *The Reader's Digest* . . .

EMIL:    Eh?

GEORGE:  Also they've found a use for cancer.

EMIL:    Knock wood.

GEORGE:  It's about time. All the millions we spend on research, cigarettes . . .

EMIL:    Wildlife.

GEORGE:  Nothing wrong with spending money on Wildlife.

EMIL:    It's all take, take, take.

GEORGE:  Nature gives it back many times over.

EMIL:    Yeah?

GEORGE:  A blue heron at sunset.

EMIL:    They're all dead . . .

GEORGE:  A whiff of breeze from the lake . . .

EMIL:    . . . or hiding.

GEORGE: A flight of Ducks.

EMIL: The duck is, after all, only a bird.

GEORGE: But what a bird.

EMIL: A pigeon, too, is a bird.

GEORGE: There's no comparison.

EMIL: What is the difference between a duck and a pigeon?

GEORGE: Basically, a lack of comparison.

EMIL: Aside from that?

GEORGE: It is a difference of . . . self-respect. You can't argue with that.

EMIL: I won't begin.

GEORGE: It wouldn't get you anywhere.

EMIL: Ha. Ha.

GEORGE: Big talk.

EMIL: I'm ready to back it up.

GEORGE: Oh yeah?

EMIL: Yeah.

GEORGE: All right.

EMIL: . . . anytime you're ready.

GEORGE: I'm ready.

EMIL: All right, then.

GEORGE: Are you ready?

EMIL: You betcha, Red Ryder.

GEORGE: Good.

EMIL: . . . Hey! What? Grownups squabbling about birds?

GEORGE: You started it.

EMIL: I beg to differ.

GEORGE: Go right ahead.

EMIL: All right, I *do* differ.

GEORGE: It makes no difference. I was holding an intelligent conversation and then you came along . . .

EMIL: And simply pointed out that you were turning something into a thing which it is not.

GEORGE: What is more noble than a duck.

EMIL: Depends on the duck.

GEORGE: Is a pigeon more noble than a duck.

EMIL: Are you saying that just because the duck is wild and has no rules . . .

GEORGE: No rules? No rules? No rules but the sun and the moon! No rules but the law of the seasons and when to go where at what specific time? No rules but to find a mate and cleave into her until death does him part?

EMIL: Is that true?

GEORGE: It surely is.

EMIL: That I didn't know.

GEORGE: Well, learn from your mistakes.

EMIL:     I will.

GEORGE:   No rules!

EMIL:     All right.

GEORGE:   One of the most rigid creatures.

EMIL:     I'm sorry.

GEORGE:   Did you know that many human societies are modeled on those of our animal friends?

EMIL:     Pish.

GEORGE:   I beg to differ about it.

EMIL:     Pish foo.

GEORGE:   The French, for example.

EMIL:     Are modeled on animals?

GEORGE:   Historically, yes.

EMIL:     Where did you get that?

GEORGE:   Some guide to France.

EMIL:     I don't believe it.

GEORGE:   I got it somewhere, I'll show you.

EMIL:     You do that.

GEORGE:   I will.

EMIL:     You just do that.

GEORGE:   Don't push me.

EMIL:     I won't.

GEORGE:   All right.

EMIL:     Darn tootin'.

# "Whenever I Think Of Wild Flying Things"

EMIL: Whenever I think of wild flying things I wonder.

GEORGE: Yes?

EMIL: If, in the City, as we are . . .

GEORGE: Yes?

EMIL: We maybe . . .

GEORGE: Yes?

EMIL: Forget it.

GEORGE: Ducks.

EMIL: Ducks.

GEORGE: Ducks. Flying wild.

EMIL: Wild over boundaries.

GEORGE: Lakes, rivers.

EMIL: Imaginary lines . . .

GEORGE: The Equator.

EMIL: Never minding . . . Never stopping . . .

GEORGE: Stopping for no man.

EMIL: High above unmanned terrain.

GEORGE: Barren.

EMIL: Unexplored North Country.

GEORGE: Naked. Strange.

EMIL: Here and there a Mountie.

GEORGE: Cold.

EMIL: Nowhere to rest.

GEORGE: What a life.

EMIL: Sleeping on the fly.

GEORGE: Blown by storms.

EMIL: You know, that is not a laughing matter . . .

GEORGE: Who's laughing?

EMIL: Much wildlife is, I am about to tell you, killed each year in storms and similar . . . things where they have a lot of wind.

GEORGE: Don't I know it.

EMIL: Another countless danger for the duck.

GEORGE: Frost, too.

EMIL: Hail.

GEORGE: Uh.

EMIL: Can you imagine it?

GEORGE: . . . Hail . . .

EMIL: Pelting the poor creature. Alone in the sky. Many feet in the air. He can't go right, he can't go left. . . .

GEORGE: Nowhere to go.

EMIL: Hail all over. Hitting him. Pelting him. Making ribbons of his wings. Creaming him out of the sky.

GEORGE: The Law of Life.

EMIL: That's what you say *now*.

GEORGE: Some must die so others can live.

EMIL: But they must die, too.

GEORGE: So some must die so others can live a little longer. That's implied.

EMIL: And then *they* die.

GEORGE: Of course. So that others can live. It makes sense if you think about it.

## THIRTEENTH VARIATION
# "They Stuff Them"

EMIL: They stuff them.

GEORGE: Eh?

EMIL: They stuff them. They shoot them and they stuff them.

GEORGE: So long as they're dead.

EMIL: Sawdust. And they tack 'em on the wall.

GEORGE: Also they stuff 'em for the oven.

EMIL: That too.

GEORGE: Yeah.

EMIL: But to kill for no reason . . . without rhyme or reason . . . to shoot them. What a waste.

GEORGE: Yes.

EMIL: What a waste in the life of a duck. To be shot. And not even eaten. Shot. Shot down like some animal.

GEORGE: At least they shoot 'em in the air.

EMIL: Huh?

GEORGE: Yeah! What do you think? You can't shoot 'em on foot? What!?

EMIL: Yeah?

GEORGE: They got *laws*. Seasons. Didn't you ever hear of Duck Season?

EMIL: Of course.

GEORGE: Well, duck season is when you can kill 'em. Legally.

EMIL: And when is it?

GEORGE: Duck season?

EMIL: Yeah.

GEORGE: Uh, the spring. Several weeks . . . The fall several weeks.

EMIL: . . . whenever the duck *is around!*

GEORGE: No, it's . . .

EMIL: Eh?

GEORGE: No, I . . .

EMIL: *Eh?*

GEORGE: Well . . . ?

EMIL: *EH?*

GEORGE: . . . yeah!

EMIL: They got the season so the only time it's not legal to shoot 'em is when they *ain't here.* . . . yeah.

EMIL: They're no dummies.

GEORGE: Yeah.

EMIL: Influence . . . strings.

GEORGE: It ain't cheap to hunt ducks.

EMIL: Are you kidding me?

GEORGE: No. You need land.

EMIL: You need a *lot* of land.

GEORGE: At least a mile. And you need . . .

EMIL: Guns.

GEORGE: One gun only.

EMIL: And a spare.

GEORGE: And some ammo to put *in* the gun.

EMIL: Telescope.

GEORGE: And those hats.

EMIL: A blatter to call them.

GEORGE: Not always necessary.

EMIL: But good to have in an emergency. . . . A bag to put them in.

GEORGE: Big boots.

EMIL: A raincoat.

GEORGE: A radio.

EMIL: You gotta take lunch.

GEORGE: You need a lotta things.

EMIL: A license.

GEORGE: And a *lot* of luck.

EMIL: Oh, yes.

GEORGE: It's easy to pick out a little wobbling duck from miles in a clear blue sky?

EMIL: No.

GEORGE: A *LOT* of luck.

EMIL: And practice.

GEORGE: Who's got the time?

EMIL: Every day. A half hour anyway. Practicing . . .

GEORGE: . . . is where they separate the men from the boys. At that moment there is no turning back. You're committed. You've been blatting around and searching the sky and crouching 'till your back hurts. From dawn on.

EMIL: Yes.

GEORGE: Lying on the cold Earth, trying not to look like anything. Hoping. Praying for that ONE DUCK . . .

EMIL: A low flying duck . . .

GEORGE: That one chance to show what *dreams* are made of. Until . . .

EMIL: Yes?

GEORGE: Until . . . off in the distance. *Beyond* the horizon 'til you don't even know what it is, is a honking. The honking comes closer. Closer and louder. You see a far-off blur. The blur becomes a speck. The speck gets bigger. It's a big speck. It's a dot. The dot is advancing and it's honking and the honking is louder and becomes clear and precise. You can just make it out. Flapping.

Flying straight in a line to join its comrades. Frantic. Lost. Dangerous. Vicious: A DUCK. . . . and on he comes. You quietly raise from the ground. One knee . . . two knees. You lift the gun, you put the gun on your shoulder and point it at the duck. It's you and him. You and the duck on the marsh. He wants to go home and you want to kill him for it. So you fire the gun. Once, again. Again. Again. Your ears are ringing. Your eyes are covered in spots. You cannot see. You are quivering and you gotta sit down. Your heart is going fast. . . .

EMIL: Where's the duck?

GEORGE: . . . slowly. Slowly you lower yourself to the Earth. Your joints creak . . .

EMIL: *Where's the duck?*

GEORGE: . . . with the weight of your body. Your shoulder aches from pounding, and your . . .

EMIL: *WHERE'S THE DUCK?*

GEORGE: The duck is dying.

EMIL: Out in the marsh.

GEORGE: Out in the marsh.

EMIL: Oh no.

GEORGE: In a flock of feathers and blood. Full of bullets. Quiet, so as not to make a sound. Dying.

EMIL: Living his last.

GEORGE: Dying.

EMIL: Leaving the Earth and sky.

GEORGE: Dying.

EMIL: Lying on the ground.

GEORGE: Dying.

EMIL: Fluttering.

GEORGE: Dying.

EMIL: Sobbing.

GEORGE: Dying.

EMIL: Quietly bleeding.

GEORGE: Thinking.

EMIL: Dying.

GEORGE: Dying, dying.

EMIL: But wait! This here! He summons his strength for one last time.

GEORGE: No.

EMIL: Maybe he beats around and tries to make it . . .

GEORGE: No.

EMIL: Back in the air?

GEORGE: No.

EMIL: One last . . .

GEORGE: No.

EMIL: A flutter of . . .

GEORGE: No.

EMIL: A little . . .

GEORGE: No.

EMIL: He's dead, isn't he?

GEORGE *nods.*

EMIL: I knew it.

GEORGE: The Law of Life.

# "For Centuries Prior To This Time"

EMIL: You know, for centuries prior to this time man has watched birds.

GEORGE: I still watch 'em.

EMIL: To obtain the secret of Flight.

GEORGE: We're better off without it.

EMIL: Yeah.

GEORGE: They'll go to their graves with it.

EMIL: The Ancient Greeks used to sit around all day looking at birds.

GEORGE: Yeah?

EMIL: Oh yes. They'd take a chair and go sit and look at 'em. Just watch them all day long and wonder.

GEORGE: I, too, would wonder. A crumbling civilization and they're out in the Park looking at birds.

EMIL: These were the Ancient Greeks. Old. Old men.
Incapable of working.
Of no use to their society.
Just used to watch the birds all day
First light to Last light.

First Light: Go watch birds.
Last Light: Stop watching birds. Go Home.
Swallows. Falcons.
Forerunners of our modern birds.
And the forerunners of our modern States.
Greeks. Birds.
Used to sit out all day long. Sit on a bench and feed them . . .
Give them little bits of . . .

GEORGE:  . . . rice?

EMIL:  Rice, yes. History is not completely clear on that point, but we can imagine rice. For the sake of argument. Rich, sleek birds of prey.

GEORGE:  And fat old men.

EMIL:  Watching each other.
Each with something to contribute.
That the world might turn another day.
A Fitting end.
To some very noble creatures of the sky.
And a lotta Greeks.